ONE WHO FINDS STILLNESS
WITHIN THE STORM
CAN NAVIGATE ANY
SEA OF SORROW.

M.C.Bell.

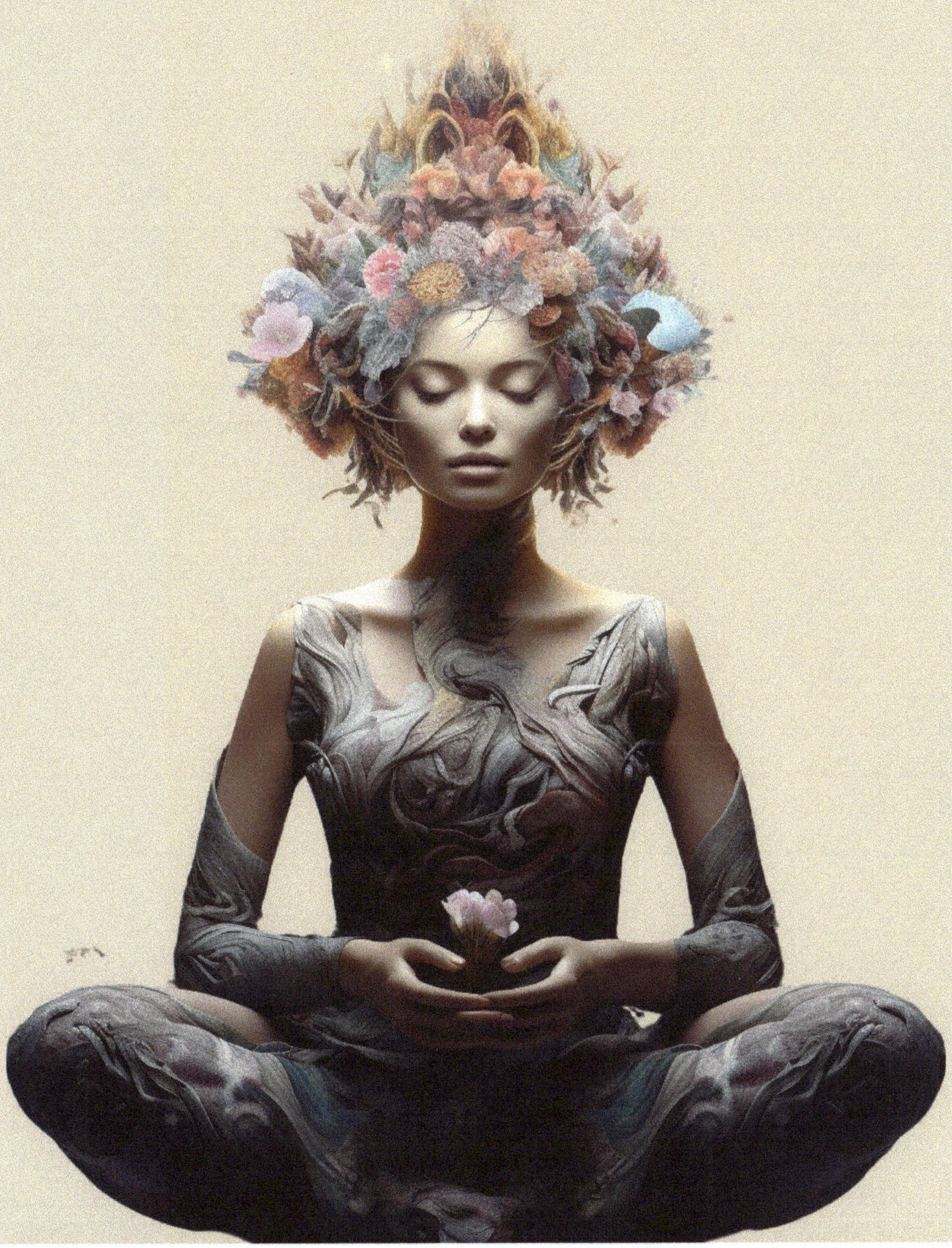

ISBN: 979-8-9902001-1-1

Printed in USA
First Edition
For permission requests, write to the publisher at the address below:
The Grief Warrior®
Visit the author's website at www.michelecynthia.com

I'm struck speechless by your generosity towards humanity and all you've given to others---your unfiltered wisdom serves a purpose reflected in your undaunted power expressed. What a powerful tribute you've created to heal the exponentially growing wounded and their losses. Everything life has handed you, you have been guided to LEAD. You are an inspiration. Your invaluable intentions are perfect in every aspect and dimension.

– ARMAND ASSANTE, Legendary Actor

From the first glance at Michele's chart, the expansive and innovative aura of her Aquarius rising is reminiscent of Walt Disney's imaginative spirit. Her persona radiates a childlike aura of love, offering warmth in today's tumultuous times. Michele, is an intuitive philosopher, she delivers universal messages that demand attention. Her planets' grounded energies, steadfast and dedicated, anchor the profound wisdom she shares. Like the stars that navigate us through the cosmos, Michele's writings serve as a celestial guide through the landscapes of healing. Her essence celebrate the perpetual cycles of transformation and enlightenment while providing solace.

– JENNY LYNCH, Celebrity Astrologer

Foundation of
EMBRACE

Prelude to Stage Two

This foundational section provides a comprehensive overview of *The 7 Stages of Grief*, setting the stage for the deep dive into **MEDITATE** that follows. While it serves as an introduction, it is designed to be revisited, offering insight and context as you navigate through each stage of your journey.

The EMBRACE Journey
Transform Grief and
Discover Inner *Strength*

Welcome, Warriors, to the extraordinary dimension of the 7 Stages of Grief Workbook Journal. I will guide you through a miraculous and empowering passage, unveiling the hidden treasures amidst the labyrinth of trauma and loss.

This course was born from my authentic desire to *heal it forward* in the grief community, ignited by theta meditation and a deep desire to manifest growth and healing through my writings. Drawing upon my intuitive theta-visions, I have created the EMBRACE framework — a radiant constellation of seven stages illuminating our transformative expedition in the wake of adversity.

In contrast to conventional approaches that merely skim the surface of emotions within the limited confines of the five stages of grief, I sensed the dire need for a holistic and transformative tapestry. The 7 stages of grief, meticulously crafted through my Healing it Forward modalities used in my 1:1 sacred retreats, transcend the ephemeral realm of emotions, ushering us into a realm where storytelling, the sacred utterance of our beloved's name, and the cultivation of gratitude mingle, guiding us through each challenging obstacle that graces our path.

Within this cherished community of kindred souls, we will unite, bound by a shared mission to collaborate, share our truth, and breathe life into one another's spirits—a sacred alchemy that fosters a radiant cascade of healing and metamorphosis. The modalities unveiled in the EMBRACE workbook journal's resplendent pages revolutionized how we navigate our sacred inner landscape, transforming the lives of those who have an unwavering longing to embrace the transformative work ahead.

As an extraordinary boon, I invite you to journey beside me as a Certified Grief Wellness Warrior, armed with the profound and purposeful modalities needed to extend a gentle hand to those ensnared in the clutches of their grief. By immersing yourself in these transformative practices and obtaining certification, you shall illuminate the path for others in their darkest moments, serving as a beacon of light and hope amidst the unfathomable abyss.

With deepest gratitude and genuine admiration, I extend my heartfelt appreciation to you for summoning the courage to embark upon the sacred journey of the EMBRACE workbook journal course. I assure you, Warriors, that this decision shall cascade with blessings and profoundly resonate. Together, let us traverse the infinite depths of grief, unlocking the wellspring of our inner fortitude and embarking upon a journey that transcends healing alone—a voyage brimming with purpose, renewal, and the willful power of the human spirit.

Prepare yourself for the transformational power of the 7 Stages of Grief Workbook Journal.

Let our extraordinary odyssey begin.

The Grief Warrior

Table of Contents

Forward 03

From My Heart to Yours 05

Prolonged Grief Disorder Unveiled 06

Unveiling the Truth: The Evolution 07

Why Prolonged Grief Disorder is Facing So Much Criticism 08

Unlock the Profound Power of Healing with EMBRACE 10

EMBRACE: The 7 Stages of Grief Alignment 12

If You're Ready To Turn Your Pain Into Fuel 14

Pivot with Purpose 15

I Had Two Choices: Retreat Or Renew 16

Our Joyful Ending: Pain Meets Healing 17

How To Sit with Your Grief 18

Are You Living a Life of Denial? 21

The Guiding Light of Embrace: Nurturing Those in Grief 22

The Healing Dance of Grief Nurturing the Spirit within 23

Why Do Some People Run When I EMBRACE My Sadness? 24

The Whispers of Compassion 25

The Unseen Language of Sorrow? Embracing Understanding 26

Unveiling the Art of Respecting Grief 28

Bottom Line 29

Does EMBRACE Speak to You? 31

Your inner spiritual warrior! 36

FOREWARD

My name is Cristal Sampson, and I work in mental health and psychiatry as a nurse practitioner in the UK, Connecticut, and New York, specializing in traumatic stress and mood disorders. I am also a young woman who experienced an early-term spontaneous miscarriage that burned a hole in depths I had previously not known existed. The revelation of this new depth of unconditional love, coupled with my baby's teeny heart stopping, left me hollow.

Even in my subsequent pregnancy the following year, I still felt empty of the unfulfillable desire for the baby back that I had lost in this life. The emptiness was filled with sadness, anxiety, and disappointment from troubled family dynamics – *a family unaware of my loss and grief.*

Someone with my expertise is never immune to the heartaches of the human experience, such as the loss of love and life. I recognized the potential to become an emotionally absent mother to my unborn baby, a fate that seemed all but certain at the time – and the thought terrified me. I am grateful to have understood that both my baby and I deserved the opportunity to heal. In my research, I discovered Michele, The Grief Warrior®.

As a health professional and a mental health specialist, I am particularly discerning about the services I opt for and the providers I choose. During this chapter of my life and given the circumstances, I did not pursue "traditional" mental health counseling. At that moment, confronting the challenges presented by contemporary therapy seemed beyond my capacity. I perceived the potential for a more conventional approach to be beneficial later in my healing journey.

What Michele provided touched the very core, breadth, and depth of my pain, reaching deep into the spiritual, mental, emotional, and energetic aspects of my being, body, and environment through a one-on-one retreat. I have not encountered anything like it since. Therefore, I am deeply moved that you are here, exploring the 7 Stages of Grief. Your journey with Michele's intentional energy, as conveyed through her books, and her custom human design modalities coupled with her healing energy, will extensively shift your essence and transform you.

FOREWARD

The 'EMBRACE: The 7 Stages of Grief' workbook series is designed to support every individual navigating grief—those who feel unprepared and overwhelmed by the complexities of losing a loved one. This series speaks to the heart of those oscillating between the anticipation of loss and the necessity of maintaining 'normalcy,' amidst the swirl of anger, resentment, and sorrow. It is a compassionate companion for every silent sufferer, for those caught in the emotional storm of impending loss, and for caregivers in dire need of nurturing themselves.

What distinguishes Michele's 'The 7 Stages of Grief' series most is the infusion of practical hope within its pages—a hope that is both tangible and deeply rooted in the natural spaces where resilience and healing begin. Michele brings a deep understanding and mastery in guiding others through the vast resources available for grief support, offering pathways that are both practical and easily navigable. Her insight into the caregiver journey, as a single mother is profoundly intimate, shaped by her own experience of lovingly supporting her teenage son, through his transition, enveloped in a cocoon of love. This unique perspective enriches her approach, making her guidance not only informed but deeply empathetic to the nuanced experiences of grief.

My work with Michele has caused a seismic shift in my perspective and has improved my relationships with myself, my family, and the people who meet me. I am moved with infinite gratitude at the positive and priceless impact my work with Michele has had on my experience of motherhood and the beautiful relationship my daughter and I get to have. Now, I enjoy expanding my connection as she has become a selfless friend and true mentor.

I encourage you to allow this book to transform you positively. Let it be a daily source of support and comfort, especially in moments of need. Remember, everything Michele has undertaken since Nicky's return to the Source has been a heartfelt ode to him and a homage to the enduring legacy of love and purpose he entrusted to her. Michele's ultimate wish is for you to discover your purpose and allow it to drive you forward through the cherished journey of your life.

Cristal Sampoon

FROM MY HEART
to yours...

Alignment in the face of loss is the only option. When we open ourselves to the possibilities presented to us, we find this harmony: in the strength of our words, in the peace of our meditations, in the gift of our presence, in the renewal of our bodies, in the stirring of our spirits, in the depth of our relationships, and in the nourishment we give ourselves.

The path to recovery is a beautiful tapestry that offers the opportunity for personal development and the forging of inner fortitude. We will brave new territory together, learn new things, and grow as people. I will be your guide and source of solace throughout our journey together. Get ready to reclaim your life with renewed confidence as you learn to swiftly navigate life's complications and unleash your remarkable inner potential.

There is nothing scary or complicated about this course since I will be there to guide you through every one of the steps. Let's take off on a journey into the unknown, where the payoff to SELF could be infinite.

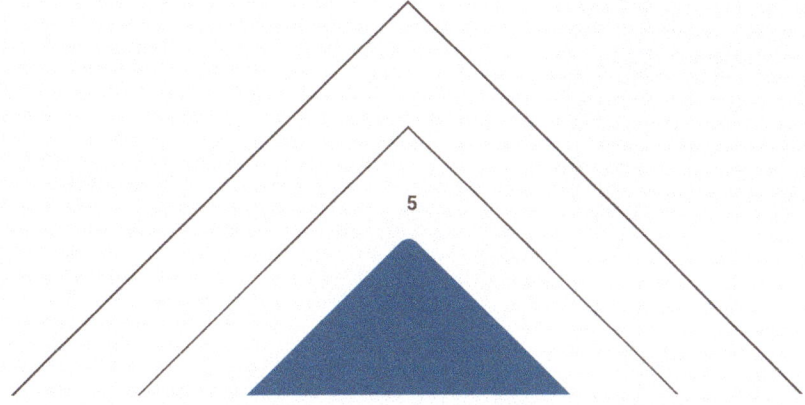

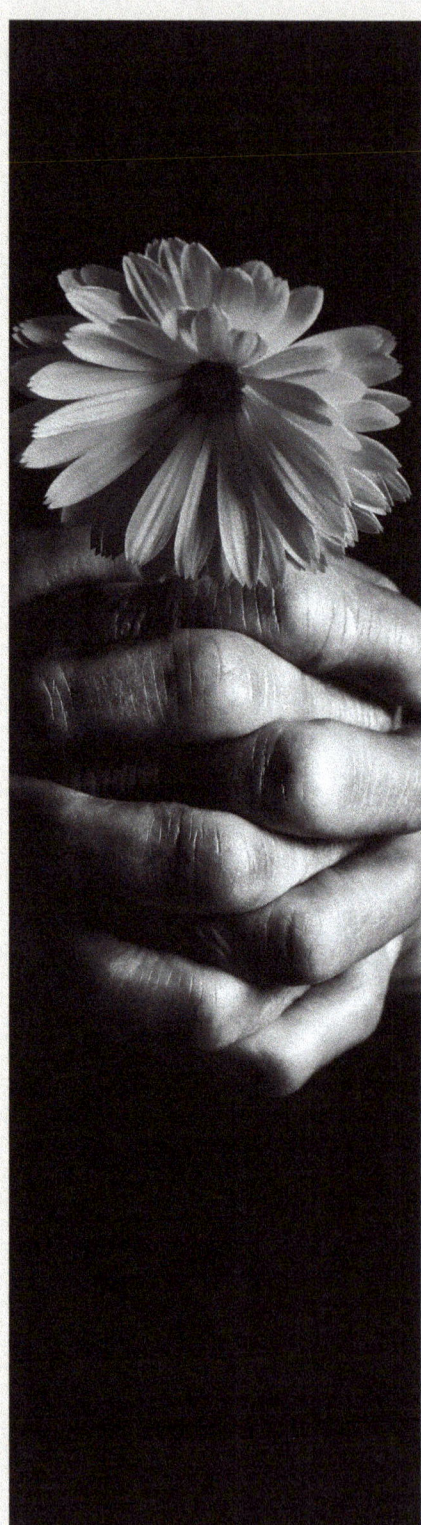

PROLONGED GRIEF DISORDER
Unveiled
as total B.S

Shattering the Illusion: Liberating Ourselves from the Constraints of the "5 Stages of Grief"

Adhering to established norms is a delusion, a fallacy we must quickly let go of when dealing with extended grief disorder. The "5 Stages of Bereavement" model developed by psychologists has been widely disseminated for too long, permeating every aspect of grief counseling and education.

Unfortunately, the constant push to conform to a set and narrow path of grieving has led me and countless other seekers within the grief community to feel disillusioned.

I beg you to disregard this erroneous advice immediately. The core meaning of our name, "EMBRACE," contains the whole truth. The concept of "Prolonged Grief Disorder" is 100% bogus.

The "5 Stages of Grief" concept originated from an unsupported theory meant to characterize the reaction of people who had been given fatal diagnoses rather than those who were navigating the maze of loss and sorrow. Here we have two utterly dissimilar yet actual experiences, each of which calls for special attention and comprehension.

UNVEILING THE TRUTH

The Evolution from
5 Stages of Grief to
Prolonged Grief Disorder

In March 2022, a new grief-related disorder was officially adopted into mainstream mental health diagnosis nomenclature. Seeing how the clinical world has further shamed the sacred grieving world is disheartening. DSM-5's trauma and stress-related category have a new label: Prolonged Grief Disorder, created deliberately to define what grief should and should not look like.

But first, let's take a moment to think. What exactly is this thing called "Prolonged Grief Disorder"? Claiming a year for adults and a paltry six months for children is an arrogant attempt to restrict the complex fabric of grief inside the confines of time. According to the American Psychological Association, persons who carry this label are assumed to exhibit the following symptoms even after the diagnostic window has closed:

- The crushing weight of grief pressed down on every aspect of their being.
- An unending fixation on sorrow as memories of the lost reverberate ceaselessly.
- A mental panorama obscured by agony or the unsettling absence of feeling.
- They engage in a delicate dance of denial and avoidance as they try to face their loved one's death.
- Dissonance and disconnection can develop when one feels different from the social norm.
- Every breath is filled with the haunting repercussions of despair and isolation.

We stand at the intersection of societal, cultural, and religious expectations, where the mere fulfillment of established criteria has become pivotal in making a prognosis. Understandably, when engulfed by the darkness of losing a loved one, such clinical classifications may not bring the peace and comprehension one wants.

To promote genuine healing, we need to permit ourselves to explore our inner emotional landscape freely.

Let us stand up as one in our resolve to overcome this stereotype's obstacles. Let us regain our freedom from societal norms to grieve and heal as we see fit.

We will overcome obstacles as a group and EMBRACE the journey of getting to the heart of our pain and reclaiming our ways forward in healing.

WHY PROLONGED GRIEF DISORDER
is Facing So Much Criticism

There is no moral compass in the arena of mourning.

Grief isn't reducible to a single feeling but incorporates many of them. It weaves a complex and ever-changing mosaic of emotions, including sadness, rage, anguish, loneliness, reverence, connection, and perplexity.

It's a shared adventure that everyone does on their terms.

Grief is complex and multifaceted: No two souls mourn alike, for no two losses are identical. Attempts to confine the grieving process within cookie-cutter stages, rigid criteria, and prescribed timelines propagate the fallacy of a right or wrong way to grieve.

Grief, in its essence, is a natural phenomenon—

A sacred dance that unfolds within the depths of our being. It is a deeply personal and profound experience, far from being a pathological problem to be solved.

A child's heart carries the imprint of a parent's absence for months or years. Similarly, a parent's longing for a child, partner, or loved one transcends all notions of time. The ache, the longing, lives in the very essence of our human nature.

Grief is an enigmatic path; Grief isn't linear.—

If we were to create a line graph of our grief journeys, it would be surprising for scientists to discover no discernible pattern.

Within the ebb and flow of our grief, we encounter good and bad days interwoven in a twisted dance.

Embracing this is how we move with our grief. Labeling and attempting to confine it only breeds resistance. Progress lies *not* in imposing a specific timeline but in surrendering to the ever-changing flow of our grief and learning to move on with acceptance and dignity.

04

Grief isn't inherently harmful.

Grief is evidence of love lost.

It serves as a poignant symbol of our love, our desire to cherish and remember those individuals and relationships that hold deep significance in our lives.

It's instinctively human: both beautiful and painful. By labeling grief as a problem in this sacred space, By labeling grief as a problem to solve, we carry it. By leaning into our pain, we *move with* it.

05

Grief looms of isolation. Support becomes our lifeline.

Grief defies measurement, transcending the confines of milestones as the 5 Stages of Grief imply. It is an ever-evolving journey, an ongoing experience. Pathologizing and diagnosing grief makes it feel abnormal. In reality, it represents so much of the human experience.

Diagnoses can empower us by illuminating how our minds or bodies function differently and offering solutions. However, diagnosing grief only deepens the shame, loneliness, and isolation. No one should feel wrong for grieving beyond a specific date.

We need grief support, not grief diagnosis. By creating space for its expression, allowing its capacity to unfold without restraint.

Unlock the Profound Power of Healing with EMBRACE
The 7 Stages of Grief Alignment

Are you prepared to immerse yourself on a journey of healing and self-discovery?

Step into a sphere of authenticity, truth, and love as you immerse yourself in the unparalleled wisdom and guidance offered in the transformative EMBRACE course. This course goes beyond the ordinary, offering a depth of healing that will leave an indelible impact.

What sets EMBRACE apart? It emerges from the heart of an expert grief practitioner, infused with the spirit of authenticity and infused by a genuine desire to empower and support individuals on their unique healing journeys.

EMBRACE offers a transformative approach that transcends traditional teachings.

Through this meticulously crafted course, you will unlock the tools and techniques to navigate the depths of grief, embracing healing and growth. The 7 Stages of Grief Alignment workbook becomes your trusted companion, providing compassionate guidance through each stage. It empowers you to honor your journey, embrace your emotions, and pave the way for a purposeful shift.

However, EMBRACE's path forward still needs to be completed. Those interested in learning more and becoming certified "Healing it Forward" practitioners will find that this course provides a beautiful opportunity to do just that. As a trained professional, you will be honored to assist others on their journey to wholeness and personal development.

The EMBRACE program is an astonishing journey of self-discovery and empowerment, not simply another healing class. It encourages you to look within, where you'll find the key to your inner wisdom and the key to your recovery. Along the journey, you'll be surrounded and transformed by a community of like-minded spirits who share your unyielding dedication to growth and give support and encouragement.

Are you prepared to take your life's most incredible life-changing healing journey? Join us on this life-altering adventure, where our north stars are sincerity, honesty, and love. Learn the true meaning of pivoting with intent through your experience with EMBRACE. Your healing journey awaits, and we are here to walk alongside you every step of the way.

Are You Ready?

ALL RIGHT, GRIEF WARRIORS:

We're breaking up with the 5 Stages of Grief

Meet your new boo,
the 7 Stages of Grief Alignment!

The 7 Stages of Grief Alignment knows no order. They are not
steps but continual pillars, symbols, and actions to make
space for grief in your growth.

Words hold immense power, and we choose to
transform our grief rather than diagnose it.

The Grief Warrior

EMBRACE

THE 7 STAGES OF GRIEF ALIGNMENT

01

EXPRESS

Let your emotions guide you and experience the joy and fulfillment of expressing your true self through journaling and artistic exploration.

02

MEDITATE

Embrace the power of sitting with your grief, opening your heart, and leaning into the serenity of the present moment, creating space for healing and growth.

03

BE PRESENT

Pause. Observe and relinquish the need for constant busyness, and tune into the depths of your feelings. Embrace the beauty, opportunity, and purpose in this moment.

04

REJUVENATE

Reignite your zest for life, nourish your soul, and elevate your vibrations through the transformative power of self-care. Rediscover what it means to feel truly alive.

05

AWAKEN

Awaken the part of you that's been hiding. Reclaiming lost joy, energy, and vibrance. Rediscover the essence of your true self, waiting to be revealed.

06

CONNECT

Grief can separate us from true ourselves, making us feel like trapped observers of our lives. Reconnect physically, mentally, and spiritually to find your center and regain a sense of control and profound connection.

07

EAT HEALTHY

Nourish your body with the fuel it craves for strength and vitality. Embrace the sensory delight of flavors, textures, and intuitive connection as your body receives each healthy bite.

What 'stage' speaks to you?

IF YOU'RE READY TO TURN YOUR PAIN INTO FUEL...

Your past can lead you to your purpose.

Your pain can become your fuel to embody and fulfill that purpose. It's time to heal the resilient spirit within you, the one who has overcome more than imagined possible.

Unclench your jaw. Let out a sigh of relief - and stop running. We can't change our pasts. e may not alter our pasts, but we can find peace in our history and shape our futures by nurturing our souls in the present moment.

Each of us possesses a unique narrative shaped by our experiences. While we may not always have control over the plot, we have the power to choose the underlying theme. Let us craft our stories around the essence of healing rather than being defined by pain.

Rise as a warrior, not just a survivor. I am here to guide you because I believe in your strength.

It's time to take hold of the reins and chart a path toward healing, love, and inner strength.

i believe in you.

Your past paves the path to purpose.

Grab a pen, and we'll embark on your new journey together.

PIVOT *with* PURPOSE

My vocation is a sacred calling, where every word, line, and page is carefully crafted with intention and purpose. My vocation extends far beyond the conventional realms. It transcends the boundaries of traditional academia and ventures into the realm of energy and transcendence.

Having traversed the depths of deep trauma and loss, I intimately understand the weight of grief and despair. Yet, I alchemize that suffering into meaning through the art of writing, creating, and teaching. I am fueled by authentic and intentional love in every breath of my life.

It is not a love born out of obligation but a love that empowers and inspires, beckoning others to rise above their fears and embrace the limitless possibilities that lie within them.

To me, this is the very essence of sacredness.

Let this inspire you that, no matter your challenges, you can *Pivot with Purpose* and manifest life in alignment with your highest energy. As your Grief Warrior® mentor, I will guide you on a sacred transformation journey.

I HAD TWO CHOICES:
Retreat Or Renew

When my first-born son passed away, grief consumed me. I could have withdrawn from life, but a fire within me refused to give up. It was then that I realized grief is the expression of love. It's our mind and heart's way of grappling with loss. It requires embracing the unknown, for life itself is unpredictable, regardless of our beliefs.

In rediscovering the magic of life, I rekindled my commitment to live truly. The grief didn't vanish, but it became more manageable. I started noticing the small things that bring joy to life. Each day became an adventure filled with endless possibilities. With an open heart, I welcomed the uncertainties that came my way. While the aftermath of a loss can leave us feeling hopeless, the strength to persevere can lead to unexpected achievements. Withdrawing may seem tempting, but it only perpetuates a downward spiral. We can move forward and rediscover joy by renewing our commitment to purposeful living.

I crafted the 7 Stages of Grief Alignment to renew my commitment—a guide from eleven years of personal experience and introspection. My book, A Son's Gift, became a testament to living intentionally after unforeseen circumstances. This challenge navigates the unexpected tragedies that may befall us, particularly if we face intense grief for the first time. Each stage holds significance, and we must traverse them daily. It isn't always easy, but a life infused with meaning and purpose is worthwhile.

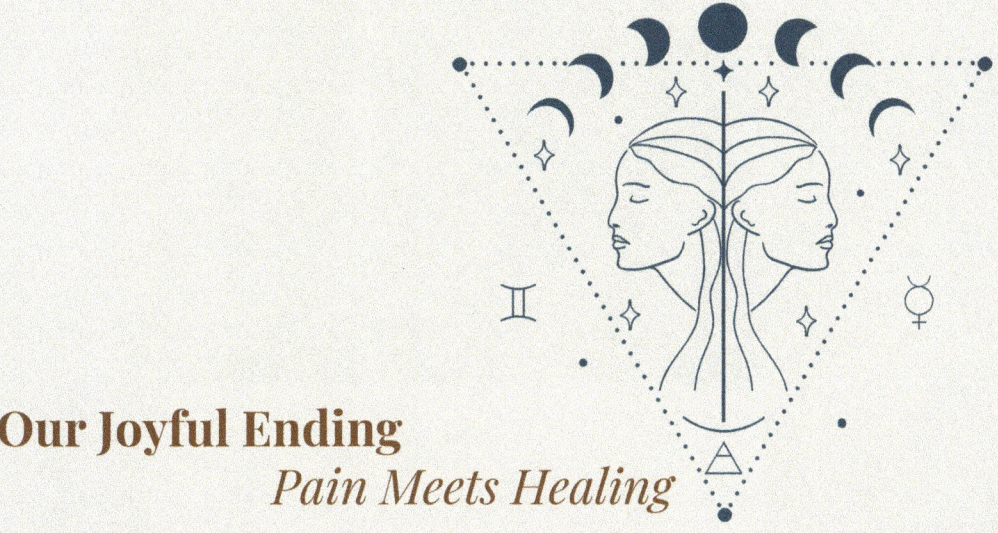

Our Joyful Ending
Pain Meets Healing

Once upon a time,

...in the whimsical land of Serenityville, a group of courageous warriors known as the Serene Seekers set forth on a remarkable quest—the Journey of Healing it Forward. Guided by the wise and enchanting fairy Seraphina, they discovered the secret power of acceptance. The goal was to align with the 7 Stages of Grief and release the mystical power inside.

The Serene Seekers set out on their journey full of bravery and love. As they wandered through enchanted forests and sparkling waterways, they experienced times of hardship. They didn't shy away since they knew the answer to their problems resided within themselves.

The Serene Seekers blazed a trail based on the ancient wisdom of the 7 Stages of Grief Alignment. Each phase—"Express," "Meditate," "Be Present," "Rejuvenate," "Awaken," "Connect," and "Eat Healthy"—held a vital piece of the puzzle to their recovery and development.

Under Seraphina's guidance, the Serene Seekers learned that pain was not their enemy but a teacher to be embraced. It became a part of their story, a testament to their courage and resilience. United in their journey, they supported one another, sharing stories and offering solace when needed. Their empathy and compassion wove a love web across Serenityville.

By embracing their pain, the Serene Seekers discovered the profound magic of healing it forward. They realized their healing could inspire and uplift others, spreading hope and resilience far and wide.

The Serene Seekers' journey through the 7 Stages of Grief Alignment showcased the power of acceptance and showed the world how beautiful it can be. Their travels exemplified the concept of "healing it forward," the idea that one person's kindness may positively impact others.

And so, the Serene Seekers continued their noble quest, fueled by determination and love. Together, they embarked on the Journey of Healing It Forward, embracing their pain, sharing their stories, and spreading seeds of healing throughout Serenityville and beyond.

This uplifting tale illustrates the power of facing our suffering and moving with "Healing it Forward."

HOW TO
Sit *with* Your Grief

ACKNOWLEDGE IT.

OWN IT.

EXPLORE IT.

THERE ARE *3* FUNDAMENTAL

STEPS TO EMBRACING YOUR GRIEF

FEEL *and*
ACKNOWLEDGE IT

Feel - Dive into the Depths of Emotion In the first step. We will learn the art of feeling. Relax your body and mind by closing your eyes and taking a few slow, deep breaths. Don't oppose or judge the feelings you're experiencing.

Are you on the verge of purging, overwhelmed by a storm of pain, guilt, shame, betrayal, or envy?

In EMBRACE, you will understand the depth of your pain through emotional exploration. Embracing our feelings shows respect for the integrity of our experience and lays the foundation for healing.

To *acknowledge* is to embrace the power of acceptance with the courage to feel. It is easy to dismiss our grief, burying it beneath layers of denial or self-judgment. But this step teaches us to embrace our pain by acknowledging its presence. Let go of the urge to push your feelings aside or berate yourself for struggling. Instead, recognize that grief is a natural and valid experience. When you own your suffering, you allow yourself the time and perspective to determine what's causing it.

OWN YOUR FEELINGS
of Pain, Grieving, Loss

Understanding your feelings is the first step, but owning your pain is crucial. Grief is often associated with a side of ourselves that we prefer to ignore, so we dismiss it. However, pushing your emotions aside or criticizing yourself for struggling can worsen things. Instead, it's essential to accept your pain as a natural and valid experience and take responsibility for it.

By holding yourself accountable, you can create the space and understanding necessary to delve deeper into the issue and uncover its root cause. This process of self-exploration allows you to work with your pain rather than fighting against it, leading to gradual healing and release from its grasp. With time, you may find that your pain becomes a source of wisdom and inspiration, helping you cultivate self-compassion, acceptance, and strength.

So, don't dismiss your pain or judge yourself for feeling it. Embrace it as an opportunity for self-discovery and growth, and let it guide you on your journey.

ARE YOU LIVING A LIFE *of Denial*?

Denial is a tempting refuge, an escape from facing the truth that awaits us. But is it truly living?

Yet, in denying our true selves, we rob life of its vibrant colors. We become sleepwalkers, traversing existence without truly seeing or experiencing its wonders. Disconnected from our emotions, we numb ourselves to the essence of our being, avoiding the aspects of life we dare not confront.

Grief has a way of leaving us feeling empty, disconnected from the world. Faced with such turbulent emotions, it is crucial to remain present. Opening ourselves to the surrounding reality allows us to reestablish our connection to ourselves and the world surrounding us.

If denial has become your shield for too long, it is time to confront the truth. Though it may be a painful pilgrimage, evading your emotions and sidestepping the obstacles that impede your growth will only perpetuate your suffering. To live a life of integrity and authenticity, we must be brave enough to acknowledge our wounds and fears.

Embrace the journey, for it may come with its share of challenges. Remember, transformation is not an overnight process; it requires time and intense dedication. But as you courageously confront your pain, you will uncover hidden wells of strength within. Say goodbye to denial and welcome the truth of your existence. With each intentional step, you carve a path toward a life filled with authenticity and purpose.

The path ahead may be arduous, but you are not alone. I am here to offer my unwavering support, accompanying you through every stride of this transformative journey. Embrace your inner resilience and have faith in the healing process.

Trust yourself and step boldly into a life of authenticity and growth. You have the power to rewrite your story.

The Guiding Light of *Embrace* Nurturing Those in Grief

Faced with another's grief, we often find ourselves at a loss for words. The profound pain and sorrow they bear can leave us powerless, uncertain of how to offer solace in their darkest hours. Yet, amidst the vastness of this challenge, there exists a flare of hope—a well-crafted grief book, EMBRACE.

In these pages, you'll find a companion journal that will bring comfort and understanding to those roaming the twisted path of sorrow.

While it is impossible to erase the pain, EMBRACE can soothe the aching heart and guide one's steps through the obstacles of grief.

The sentimental narratives make the emotions' kaleidoscope more explicit and the burden of grief more tolerable. As a treasured tool in your grief bag, the 7 Stages of Grief Alignment provides a roadmap for the griever and their companions, fostering awareness and healing.

Yet, it is crucial to remember that when supporting someone living in grief, the gift of your presence and enduring willingness to listen outweighs any words of wisdom or reassurance.

With its intricate nuances, grief often leaves those who mourn feeling isolated and misunderstood. EMBRACE is a heartfelt promise that assures you that you are not alone in your journey.

EMBRACE will offer hope and encouragement, reminding readers they are not alone in their sorrow. Consider giving them a copy to support a friend or loved one during grief.

If you want to support a friend or loved one during grief, consider giving them a copy of EMBRACE! You want the support of your loved ones, and the same goes for them needing you. As with any journey in life, the journey of grief as a team, we got this!

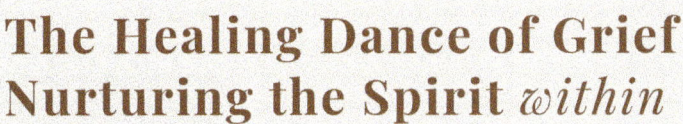

The Healing Dance of Grief
Nurturing the Spirit *within*

When someone close to us dies tragically, we are engulfed by an overwhelming sense of loss, accompanied by a symphony of painful emotions. We journey through this dimension of grief, uniquely navigating its twists and turns. Some shed tears like raindrops from a stormy sky, others ignite with fiery anger, while some retreat into the solitude of their inner world. These reactions, these expressions of grief, are the rivers that flow from the depths of our souls. We must honor them, for within these expressions lie the seeds of self-awareness and the catalysts for healing.

It's simple to feel disoriented and overwhelmed in today's fast-paced, ever-evolving society. The grieving process is a multifaceted test; we all long for the loving company of a compassionate that requires us to seek comfort from those who can relate. As a holistic practitioner, I stand ready with the tools and resources to accompany you on this sacred pilgrimage. Drawing upon my extensive experience, I offer a sanctuary where your voice can be heard, your story shared, and your healing ignited.

Discerning the way forward is exhausting in life's chaotic orchestra, where confusion and uncertainty reign. The weight of emotional pain may tempt us to forge ahead, mindlessly seeking an escape from the obstacles that hinder our progress. Yet, dear soul, a profound wellspring of resilience and strength lies within you. Developing spiritual growth can lead to a limitless abundance of peace and stability. Nurturing your connection with a higher power or the wisdom within you can help you navigate life's most brutal storms with grace and serenity. As you enter this sacred journey of spiritual expansion, you will uncover newfound capacities to navigate life's turbulent seas, supporting your passage and extending a loving hand to those who traverse similar paths.

The road may appear dimly lit as you tread its winding path. Yet, within you resides a radiance of faith, highlighting the darkness for those who desire comfort in your presence. Even when grief looms, keep hope alive in the sanctuary of your heart. I encourage optimism even in the darkness. Envision a shining star, your inner strength shining its light into the deepest crevices of despair. As you gaze upon the darkness, challenge fear and vulnerability to manifest and transform into a conduit for healing. By embracing the full spectrum of your being, shadows, and all, you control the destiny of self-empowerment. Even in the trenches of darkness, your intense light inspires and uplifts those who witness your strength and courage.

Remember that you are never alone in the sacred dance of grief, where each step is steeped with the essence of unconditional love. Reach out, Warrior, to those who can guide and support you on this transformative pilgrimage. Together, you will honor the pain, nurture your spirit, and spin a tapestry of healing that extends far beyond the realms of grief. Let the rhythm of your heart guide you, as it holds within it the tune of perseverance, the harmony of optimism, and the assurance of rejuvenation.

Shadows become tools that help shape
Who You Are...

The Symphony of *Empathy*
Navigating Responses to *Grief*

Why do some people run when I embrace my sadness?

Have you ever felt alone in your sadness because others choose to ignore or withdraw from you?

It's disheartening to question whether you deserve support or understanding. It can be challenging for those not accustomed to dealing with intense emotions like grief to face their feelings. Fear, unfamiliarity, and a lack of knowledge about responding supportively could all contribute to their feelings.

It can feel like others are trying to hide from the truth of your experience and being when they avoid hearing about your sorrowful tale. It might make you feel invisible, alone, and desperate for approval. An essential part of the grieving process is vulnerability, which searches for comfort in human connection and comprehension.

However, it is essential to note that only some can face and hold space for strong emotions, especially if they have not experienced something comparable. Their insecurity stems from a need for more ease with showing emotion. It's important not to take their reaction personally; instead, give yourself time and space to work through your feelings.

Be gentle with yourself and embrace the understanding that not everyone will comprehend or offer enduring support on this path. With time, you'll meet people who can hold the sacred space for your grief, opening doors to vital life lessons and opportunities for new relationships.

There can be many reasons why people don't respond to your melancholy expressions. Some people may struggle with displays of intense emotion, while others may feel ill-equipped to respond to someone who is deeply sorrowful. In certain instances, people may even fear that witnessing your sadness will awaken their dormant pain. It is essential to acknowledge that each person uniquely navigates grief, and adverse reactions to your sorrow do not show a lack of care or concern. Give them breathing room to deal with their feelings; they may discover the strength to help you.

As you continue your grief journey, remember that your emotions are valid and that your need for support is real. Seek solace in those who can hold space for your grief, and let go of the notion that everyone will understand. The dance of empathy requires patience and calls for self-compassion. If you care for yourself during this process, you show others how accepting melancholy can strengthen the spirit.

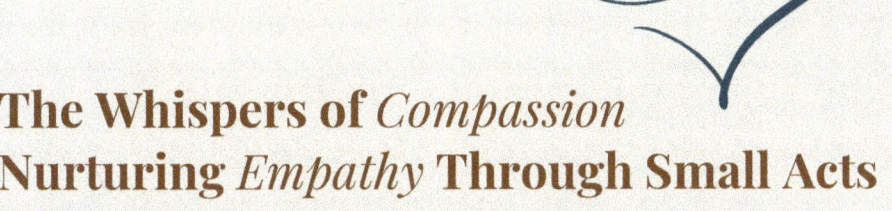

The Whispers of *Compassion*
Nurturing *Empathy* Through Small Acts

Empathy's complex webs of connection strengthen relationships during the grieving process. A kind touch, reassuring words, and a listening ear can go a long way toward alleviating emotional pain. During sadness, expressions of sympathy transform into a beautiful melody of support, kindness, and concern.

Even the tiniest gestures can convey the magnitude of affection and concern in moments of quiet reflection. Sincerity and love injected into the most straightforward actions can illuminate the darkest places. These seemingly insignificant acts go beyond words to bring solace to the soul. By doing these nice things for them, we can let them know they have our undying support and are not alone.

Sometimes, the answer lies not in words but in the silent embrace of companionship. To stand beside someone in their darkest hours to honor their wishes can transcend an act of compassion. You become a sanctuary of support for their wounded soul. Becoming a lifeline amidst the chaos by offering practical help, running errands, and preparing nourishing meals demonstrates that our warmth extends beyond mere words to sacred stillness.

They provide a sympathetic ear that accepts their suffering without judgment or making demands. We become instruments of compassion and wisdom, holding the door open for their recovery.

When words fail, being there and knowing how grateful we are can help comfort a broken spirit. Therefore, let us recognize the significance of greeting cards, reassuring embraces, and quiet moments of reflection. Aim to personify empathy, compassion, and concern. We become the vessels through which comfort is delivered, mending the broken parts of a mourning person's spirit in those quiet times.

You can use the following phrases:

My heart goes out to you; I'm sorry this is happening to you.
"What is your loved one's name?"
"What do you say we get some lunch together? Please tell me more about (insert name of cherished one here)."

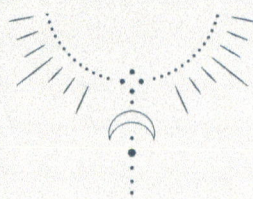

The Unseen Language of Sorrow
Embracing *Understanding* and *Letting Go*

It's frustrating when those close to you don't understand how much your loss means to you. Some wonder if avoiding those who can't share our sorrow is right. But let's PAUSE to think about this:

No matter how well you articulate your pain, not everyone can comprehend complex emotions. Despite our efforts to articulate our pain, some may struggle to grasp its true essence. In these situations, letting go of our dependence on their comprehension is not a sign of a lack of strength or inability. Our efforts to help them understand the inexplicable would be well-spent.

Don't you think it's wonderful to imagine a world where empathy is cultivated and understanding becomes a part of our collective etiquette? While that ideal may be far off, we can take comfort in the company of those who share our values and offer proper understanding and support. Seek comfort in knowing you are not alone on your grief journey. By doing so, we create space for our healing, allowing our sorrow to unfold in its way, guided by our resilience and the support of those who truly understand.

01

Let us find comfort in the arms of those who truly understand and share our pain on this developing path of sorrow. Even if others can't understand our pain, it's reassuring that some would listen with empathy and provide a safe place to heal.

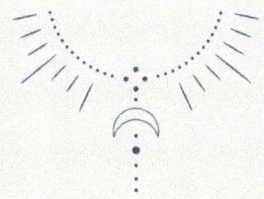

02

In the depths of sorrow, we are faced with a "griefosophical" lesson:

We are the chosen ones entrusted with the sacred duty of carrying the unseen language of sorrow. It is not a burden to bear but a calling that sets us apart from others. Our connection with our departed loved one runs deep, transcending the comprehension of others. The love we shared with them was unique, profound, and intimate, coloring our grief in hues that may mystify those who did not experience the same depth of connection.

Rather than harboring resentment or seeking understanding from those who cannot offer it, we can shift our perspective. It helps to think of ourselves as spiritual vessels that have solemnly promised to bear the burden of our grief. To mourn together is to witness the strength of love and reveal the depth of our connection.

By letting go of the expectation that everyone will understand our grief, we unlock a sense of communal understanding only discernible by our innermost beings. We become a collective source of higher consciousness. Our common grief language helps us bond with those who resonate with our vibe.

So, Warriors, Let up, hoping other people share your pain with you. Embrace the idea that you are connected to a group of people who "get it," and you become a force that cannot be stopped together. Make use of your suffering as a starting point for introspection and growth.

In doing so, you give tribute to the unconditional love you shared with your departed loved one and become that twinkle who walks this path of grief.

In grief, we are chosen to carry
the unseen language of sorrow,
a testament to our love and
resilience.

Unveiling the Art of Respecting *Grief*

In this era of digital connectivity, we find ourselves conditioned to swiftly move on and brush aside the depths of our grief. Glossing over the importance of grieving and grief acceptance might be easy in today's fast-paced world. However, grief encompasses far more than prolonged sadness; it is an emotional journey that demands time, reverence, empathy, and patience to mend.

Loss, especially the irreparable loss of love, is at the heart of mourning. When we suffer a profound loss, it changes who we are and shines a light on what gives our lives true purpose. The path to recovery and growth lies in sincerely accepting our suffering.

Nobody enjoys being hurt, and most people will try to avoid it. However, suffering is a part of being human and must be faced head-on. Grief and loss, and the emotional sorrow they cause, are experiences all humans share at some point. Neither can we expect anybody else to take away our suffering, but we can show compassion, which can teach us a great deal about how to deal with the misery of others. Through compassion, we see that the suffering of others is natural and merits our whole attention.

The ability to empathize with others serves as a helpful reminder that there is no single "correct" way to deal with suffering. It is unnecessary to have all the solutions to be compassionate; all we need to do is be there for people when they are suffering.

So, when we see a loved one going through a tough time, let's not rush to ease their suffering. Instead, let's give our undivided attention to becoming wise. By doing so, we show them the kindness and consideration they deserve. There is an act of tremendous bravery, tenacity, and grit at the heart of mourning, an act that teaches profound truths about what it is to be human. So, let's not rush past the remembrances of limitless, unconditional LOVE.

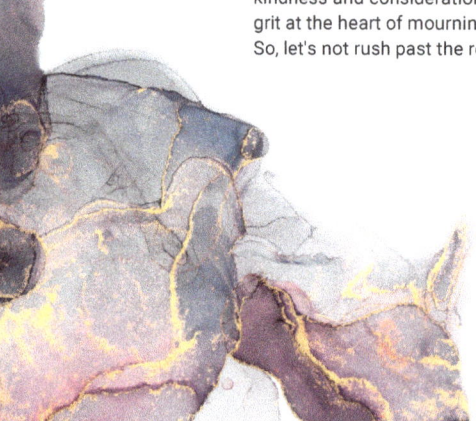

Embracing the *Everlasting* Journey

BOTTOM *line*

One of life's greatest challenges is coming to terms with the fact that mourning is never really "done." We may reach a point where the raw pain of our loss has begun to fade, but the scars remain. These scars can be a source of strength and comfort. They remind us of the loved ones we have lost and help us appreciate life's fragility.

But keep in mind that you will never fully "get over" your loss. It is an ongoing journey that we all must travel. There may be days when the path is smooth and the going is rough. But eventually, we will reach our destination: a place where we can find peace and happiness again.

Healing is an ever-unfolding journey, an intricate dance of self-discovery and growth. As we set out on our journey, we recognize that our wounds are not who we are but a testament to our capacity to love fiercely and persevere through adversity. Unconditional self-love feeds the soul and opens the door to healing on all levels. Putting aside baggage and focusing on what brings us joy might help us find inner freedom.

You may find that your relationship with your loved one changes as you move through grief. Their presence becomes a source of strength and comfort, reminding you of their eternal love. You gradually rebuild your life as you heal, carrying their memory within you. Their spirit entwines with yours, illuminating the path to a meaningful existence.

While healing may never be complete, grief can propel you toward a more positive emotional journey. Embracing and expressing your grief healthily allows for soul healing to begin.

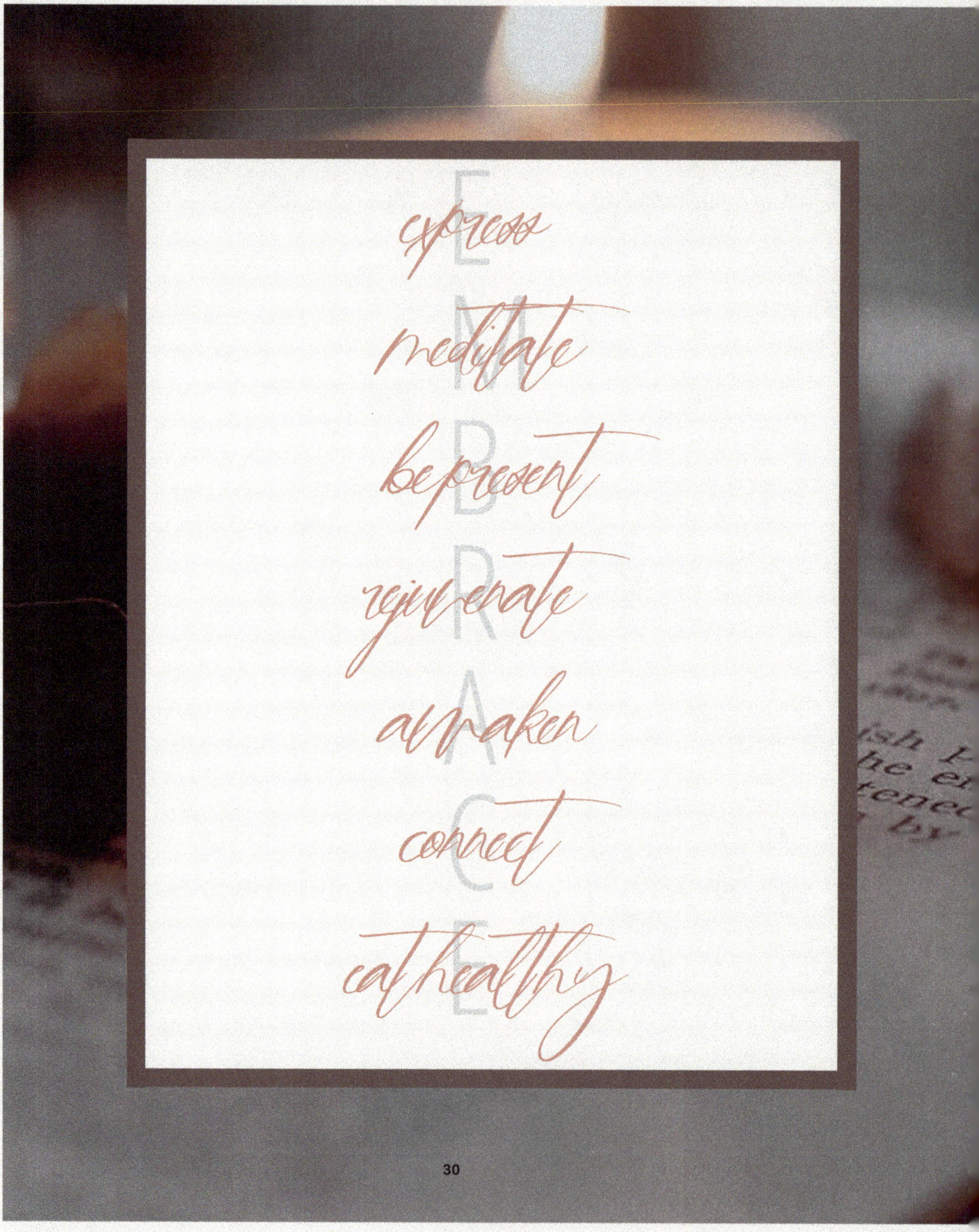

express

meditate

be present

rejuvenate

awaken

connect

eat healthy

EMBRACE

DOES EMBRACE
Speak to You?

Explore the transformative power of The 7 Stages of GRIEF Alignment workbook journal, designed to support you authentically and effectively on your grief journey. Each stage of this journal is carefully crafted to nurture your physical and mental well-being, empowering you to strengthen critical aspects of your health as you navigate through the aftermath of a traumatic event. Embracing these stages will lead you to greater strength, resilience, and a revitalized sense of purpose.

Drawing from personal experiences of loss and trauma, I created the 7 Stages of GRIEF Alignment mini journal to assist those willing to EMBRACE in their healing process. Within its pages, you'll discover practices that have deeply impacted my grief journey, enabling me to navigate through the pain and embrace genuine growth mindfully. These practices have brought about timeless healing, from releasing old attachments to rebuilding a lost sense of unconditional love.

This eternal healing perfectly captures the beauty of "Healing."

Whether at the beginning of your grief journey or making progress, embracing the stages outlined in this journal can ease the burden and infuse joy into your life. Let's say you've had enough and are ready to start living again. Please join me on the 7 Stages of the GRIEF Alignment workbook journal's transformational journey, or go even further and earn your Certified Wellness Warrior designation.

Take a deep breath, stay resilient, and remember that even in the darkest moments, we possess the inner strength to move forward. Embrace this opportunity and witness its profound impact on your life. Not doing so would be a mistake.

EXPRESS

Welcome to the First Stage of Grief Alignment: Express. In this stage, we encourage you to unleash your thoughts, feelings, and trauma through emotional journaling. By embracing this practice, you voice your emotions and release anxiety, triggers, and pain.

Reflect on its meaning in your grief journey and explore its significance. Use your notebook as a place of refuge where you may explore who you are and how you got here. Allow your own words to heal and shape your spirit.

Three ways you can integrate 'Express' into your daily therapy:

Emotional Journaling
Write freely each day to express and process your emotions.

Artistic Expression
Engage in creative activities to communicate and release emotions.

Verbal Communication
Share your feelings with a trusted person or practitioner for support and validation.

Expression is the key to unlocking our connection, allowing us to co-create a reality rooted in love and acceptance. So say their name, share your story, feel every moment, and remember—you are here for a reason. And always remember—you are here with a purpose. You have the power to create. So keep expressing yourself—you have everything it takes to thrive!

How will you express today?

MEDITATE

Have you ever explored the richness of meditation? It offers a gateway to discovering tranquility and clarity in grief or challenging moments. By dedicating time to cultivating mindful awareness, we unlock the potential for remarkable revelations.
With each intentional inhalation and exhalation, we create a sacred space within ourselves, allowing us to confront our emotions from a higher perspective.

Discover peace in nature's embrace, where meditation unveils transformative insights.

Pause for a moment and ask yourself: When was the last time you truly paused and immersed yourself in the vivid reality of "here"? It is in the here and now, the ever-present moment, where true existence lives. It is within this moment that the miracle of life unfolds.

BE PRESENT

'Be Present' is the 3rd Stage of Grief Alignment, encouraging us to be still. Society often expects us to conform to specific standards, but we have the power to within ourselves begin a path toward wellness simply by showing up.

Being present allows us to reconnect with life, love, and feel again.

Let's focus on being present and mindful. Pay attention to your breath - feel the rise and fall of your chest and let it move like a symphony's crescendo. Focus on the present and feel the caress of each inhale and exhale. Take in the vibrant feelings that sweep your entire being, and let them merge with the present moment.

Allowing your emotions to take over can be liberating. Accepting and working with our feelings without hesitation or judgment is crucial. Whatever those emotions may be, it's okay to feel them. Take a moment to permit yourself to step back, allowing your soul to have time within this very breath.

REJUVENATE

For true revitalization, we must turn inward and examine our bodily, mental, and spiritual states.

It can help us reclaim our vitality and lead us toward joy and fulfillment, especially when dealing with the loss of a loved one or the constant stresses of modern life. Transformation comes with self-reflection, inner growth, and healing. You have the power to do this!

By embracing new challenges and striving to grow in every aspect of our lives, we can reignite the spark and fire up our souls. So, why wait? We can rejuvenate and awaken joy at every level with determination and self-acceptance.

Reflecting on our loved ones and the gifts they gave us can also help rejuvenate our lives in their honor. Whether remembering a favorite memory or reaching out to those who supported us during difficult times, each act deepens the connection between us and our loved ones, even as they move beyond the physical world.

Ultimately, we choose how to react to grief, but by acknowledging our journey and embracing joy, we can find strength in our spirit again.

AWAKEN

In the 5th Stage of Grief Alignment, Awaken, you are invited to embrace the essence of being fully alive and anchored in the present moment. Retaining and shielding ourselves from raw emotions and harsh realities is expected in the depths of grief.

Awakening is the key that unlocks the door to our inner resilience and rekindles our faith in the truth that lies before us.

Pause and contemplate your life as it stands today. Allow this fresh perspective to offer a broader view, enabling you to observe your journey from a distance. In this introspection, you may realize that all you need lives within, and a vast expanse of possibilities awaits you on the horizon.

Let's embrace the awakening, as it acts as a catalyst that propels us forward with a renewed sense of vitality and purpose on our journey.

CONNECT

In the 'C' of EMBRACE, we find the power of connection in the 6th Stage of Grief. As we make our way through the complexities of this world, now is the moment to strengthen our connection to ourselves, our spirit, and our mind. While it may pose challenges, remember that we all thrive on daily connections.

How will you choose to CONNECT today?

Your mind. Your body. Your spirit.

Make a conscious effort to connect with yourself by dedicating just five minutes to express gratitude, a walk in nature, engaging in reflective journaling, cooking, creating, or allowing yourself to be still. Focus on self-care and self-reflection to enhance your well-being.

Tune in to your needs and honor them, for it is in these connections that true healing and growth can flourish.

EAT HEALTHY

In the final stage of our grief alignment journey, we are called to embrace the importance of nourishing ourselves through healthy eating. As we have journeyed through the different stages of grief in our course, we have learned the significance of addressing our emotional, mental, and spiritual needs. Now, we focus on the physical aspect of our well-being, recognizing that what we put into our bodies directly impacts our healing process.

Eating healthy becomes the inner thread that weaves all the stages of our grief alignment journey. By nourishing ourselves with wholesome, nutrient-rich foods, we provide our bodies with the fuel to support our healing from the inside out. We actively participate in our healing process by prioritizing foods promoting strength, vitality, and well-being.

As we continue our journey beyond grief, let us carry healthy eating lessons. Let us embrace the power of wholesome foods to support our ongoing healing and growth.

It is through this holistic approach that we can truly thrive and create a life that is vibrant, nourished, and filled with joy.

YOUR INNER
spiritual warrior!

EMBRACE is the ultimate exhilarating journey of healing and transformation. This course is not just a certification—it is a profound commitment to healing and a powerful dedication to moving forward with purpose.

We encounter countless challenges that test our resilience and tempt us to give up. Yet, deep within us lies an untapped well of strength, waiting patiently to be discovered and unleashed. This course empowers you to tap into that inner strength, unlock your full potential, and become the vessel to *healing it forward*.

The key lies in listening to your heart and trusting your instincts. By tuning into the untapped wisdom at the core of your being, you gain the clarity and guidance needed to navigate any obstacle that comes your way. With a resilient focus, you cultivate the courage and determination required to **move with** emotional barriers.

As you EMBRACE this journey, you discover that nurturing your inner world positively impacts your external world, cultivating meaningful connections with others, and investing in your self-enlightenment. The key lies in listening to your heart and trusting your instincts.

The 7 Stages of Grief Alignment will be your guiding light as you EMBRACE each stage of grief in your own time. Recognize that these stages are not linear processes; you may move back and forth between them as you navigate your unique grief journey. This flexibility allows you to honor your experience and progress at your own pace.

Are you ready to step into your power as a Certified Grief Wellness Coach?
Sign up today and trust your inner calling, take that leap of faith, and let your guiding light illuminate the path of healing and transformation for yourself and others.

A Graceful Pivot to Purpose

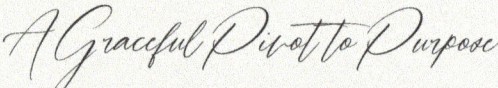

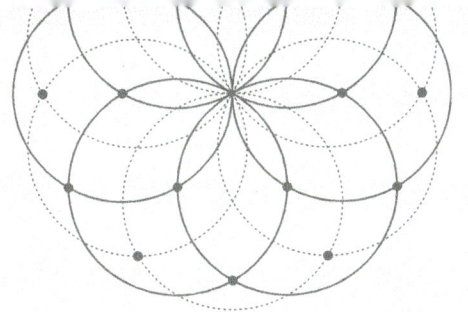

you've made it

You are now ready to **EMBRACE** our Second Stage:

— meditate —

That's the blessing and power of **pivoting with purpose.**

What are the 7 Stages of Grief Alignment?
Express. **M**editate.
Be Present. **R**ejuvenate.
Awaken. **C**onnect. **E**at Healthy.

Healing begins with acceptance, and alignment transforms us
through embracing our circumstances.

**The empowerment of embracing is in your next chapter –
are you ready to turn the page?**

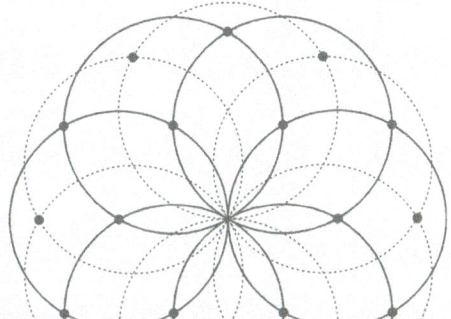

Table of Contents

Meditation 101:

How Will Meditation Guide Your Journey? 03

Trauma and Meditation: Hurting, Healing, & Hope 09

The Stages of Grief Alignment 15

Four Ways to Heal: Cultivate Positivity, Enrich it,

Absorb it, and Correlate Positivity & Negativity 22

Creating a Meditation Space for Healing 27

Healing in Action: Meditation Exercise for Trauma 33

Meditation Techniques to Transition

Purposefully Using the Body Scan Method 38

Rituals for Remembrance:

Rite of Passage Moon Meditation 45

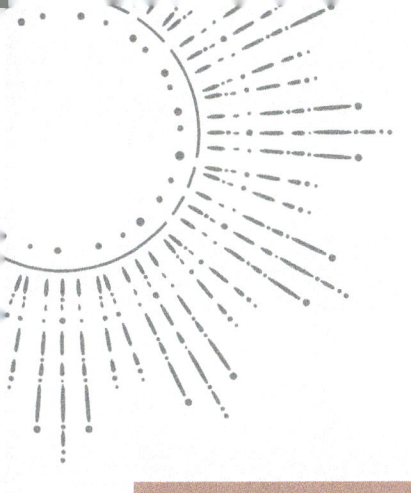

Meditation 101:
How Will Meditation Guide Your Journey?

Objective: To understand the benefits of meditation and how you can access it as a tool in your journey toward healing.

Ignite Your Warrior Spirit

Grand Rising Warriors, allow me to be your trusted guide on this next exciting chapter of your journey as you EMBRACE the possibilities. Together, we will explore, learn, and grow, allowing it all to shape us into courageous leaders with a greater understanding of our true selves!

Even when life seems overwhelming, there is still a way out. Meditation can release our burdens—anxieties, stress, memories, and trauma. By taking moments to breathe deeply, ask for assistance, and find peace in letting go, meditation allows us to refocus on what matters most: ourselves.

Why Meditation?

Since the beginning of time, humanity has sought to understand and harmonize with its internal energies through meditation. By clearing our minds of woes, we can journey towards gracefully handling external burdens - allowing us to transcend into spiritual enlightenment.

Meditation serves as a guiding light, illuminating the path to relaxation and stress relief and redirecting our focus toward the positive. It tunes us into the harmonious symphony of our inner universe, fostering a profound connection that exudes calmness and joy in our interactions with ourselves and others.

In mindfulness meditation, we step away from the chaos of our hectic lifestyles, entering a sphere of consciousness that invites relaxation, refocusing, and genuine reflection.

Meditation is a beautiful journey of self-discovery. We take time to get in touch with our innermost thoughts, feelings, and sensations without judgment or expectation. In doing so, we can transcend the stresses of day-to-day life and tap into an infinite source of peace within ourselves.

By living in the present moment, embracing silence as our trusted companion, radiating our inner light outwardly, and releasing all that obstructs our path to happiness, true healing, and contentment await us.

The Healing Benefits of Meditation

Many practitioners, coaches, and gurus have probably told you that meditation is a powerful tool for personal growth and healing.

This is a perfect example of the lovely intersection of magic and science. Here are some of the well-documented advantages that meditation can bring to your journey:

- Manage anxiety, depression, and stress (the portion of the brain responsible for regulating pressure and anxiety can shrink by regularly practicing meditation!)

- Improve your overall mood and well-being.

- You can connect with your inner self.

- Comprehend the traumas of the past and move towards your future.

- Instant sensations of healing and relief.

- Better sleep and rest.

- Sharpen your short- and long-term memory.

- You can increase your focus.

- You can explore your creative instincts.

- Improve your cognitive and problem-solving abilities.

- Support your efforts to break free from addiction by maintaining self-control.

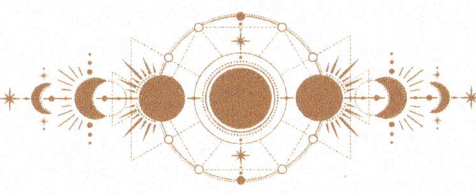

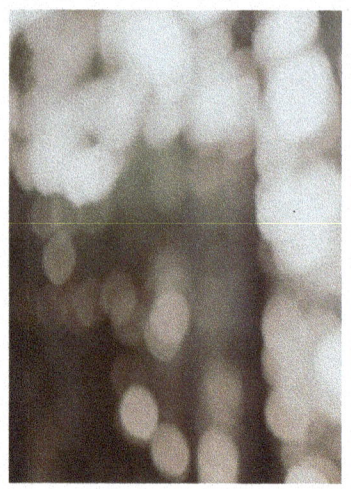

Why Will Meditation Help YOU?

- If you're here, you may be hurting.

- Maybe you've lost a child. A sibling. A friend. A loved one. Your reality feels shattered, and you're left to pick up the pieces.

- Know you're not alone in this. This pain might not go away forever, but your strength and ability to grieve and carry it in grace can empower you to move forward.

- That throughout all this pain, you can pivot with purpose. To embrace, to empower.

- It starts by looking within and honoring your emotions, learning to sit with them, and encouraging your resilience to breathe through grief, heartache, and sorrow.

- To break toxic cycles, shift your focus to the present and show yourself the gratitude, love, and care you deserve.

- It all starts with just a few meditative moments each day. Let's choose you and heal you.

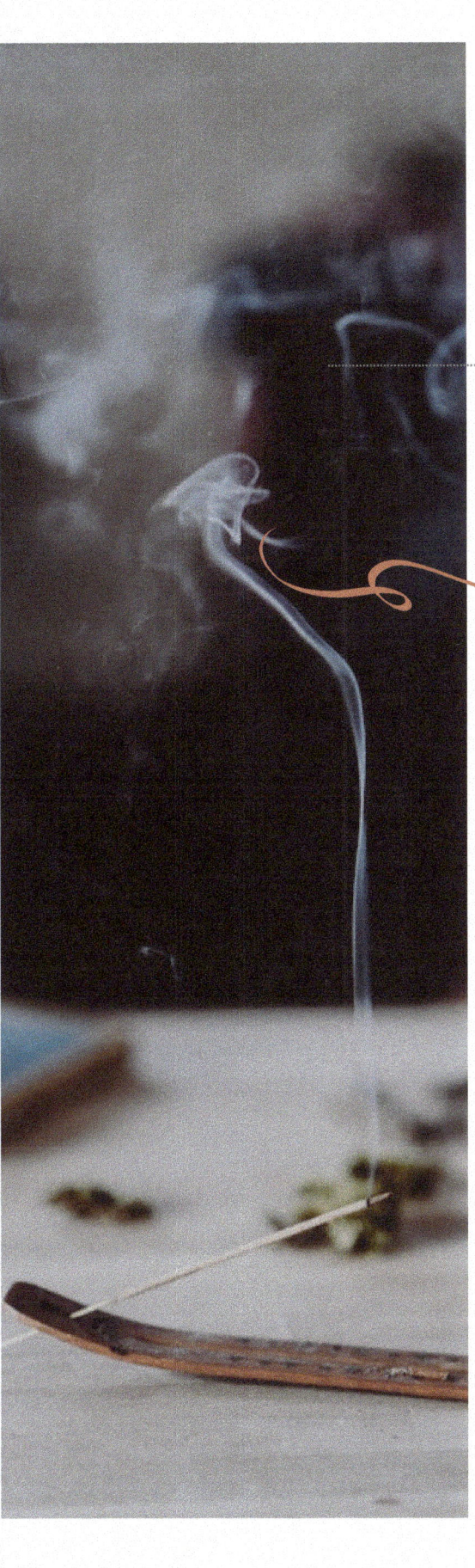

Key Points

- Meditation can help us carry and release heavy emotions, difficult memories, and traumatic experiences.

- It allows us to unwind, quiet our minds, and become at ease with the unpleasant.

- Benefits: Manage anxiety, depression, and stress; improve mood; connect with your inner self; process trauma; get instant relief; get better sleep; sharpen memory; improve focus; access creativity; improve cognition; and increase self-control.

Exercise

As we go through each chapter, please envision yourself beginning and concluding a new chapter on your journey. At the end of each chapter, I will lead you through a straightforward yet effective meditation exercise to provide immediate relief and spark your healing process.

To practice an Earthing meditation, kindly follow the instructions below:

Earthing, or grounding, is a form of meditation that can balance your energy and connect you with Mother Nature to find peace in the present moment.

It's simple: Connect with the Earth.

Try this exercise today. Find a serene location where you can unwind and relax without shoes, such as a grassy backyard or park with natural elements like dirt or rocks. Enjoy the grounding sensation and embrace the present moment.

 Be mindful of each step, walking slowly and mindfully: How does the earth feel on your skin?

 Take off your shoes and walk on the earth.

 Synchronize your breath with each step. Focus only on your breath and sensations.

 If your mind wanders, no worries. Gently shift your focus back to your breath and the earth.

 Do this for as long or as little as you please. Toward the end, express gratitude to yourself for taking the time to practice grounding.

 Now, express gratitude to the Earth and your Creator for offering you this moment of healing and beauty.

Trauma and Meditation:
Hurting, Healing, & Hope

Objective: To validate the mental and physical impact, the relationship between mindfulness and trauma, and how to let go of painful memories using meditation.

The Mental & Physical Manifestation of Loss

While death is the opposite of life, it is an inevitable part of it. And for some of us, we know the traumatic reality far sooner than we ever thought.

The feeling can be overwhelming and intense, whether it is the loss of a friend, parent, sibling, or spouse. From profound sadness to depression, shock, numbness, guilt, regret, or emptiness, the grief experience is a tumultuous sea of heavy emotions that are difficult to bear. You might even feel angry at yourself, your family, a loved one, or God. Maybe you've noticed behaviors that didn't feel right to you:

- Excessive alertness
- Continuous crying
- Avoiding social gatherings and interaction with people An urge to harm yourself
- Avoidance
- The inclination toward alcohol and substance abuse

If this is what you're feeling or experiencing, please know you're not alone. Your feelings are valid. Your experience is authentic, raw, and sometimes ruthless. And while the emotions you're carrying may seem too heavy to lift on your own, know there is hope. You are stronger than you know; life might not seem the same again, but you must focus on the future with hope and optimism to move forward.

Your health, personality, and support can strengthen you to carry your grief and move forward in growth. To pivot with purpose and embrace what's ahead of you while still honoring what's behind you.

The Philosophy of Mindfulness & Trauma

In our dance through life, the delicate art of looking forward while casting a glance back lends our journey its depth. Each soul bears the imprints of trauma differently, reminding us of the individuality of our human experience. Drawing from ancient traditions, we've turned to meditation as a profound wellspring of healing for both heart and mind.

Mindfulness is a steadfast companion in our journey through the maze of grief. It signals us not with loud proclamations but with a gentle invitation to be present and acknowledge our past's wounds. Through daily immersion in meditative reflection, we create sanctuaries of calm, pockets of peace in which our souls find rest. This awakened consciousness becomes our shield and guide, helping us cherish memories of our departed while finding the strength to continue our journey.

Healing is, in essence, a pilgrimage towards understanding our stormy seas of emotions. Instead of fleeing, facing them allows us to chart a path through the depths of our past pain toward the promise of tomorrow. In this raw vulnerability and sincere pursuit, we find the seeds of true recovery, promising us a journey filled with hope and brighter tomorrows.

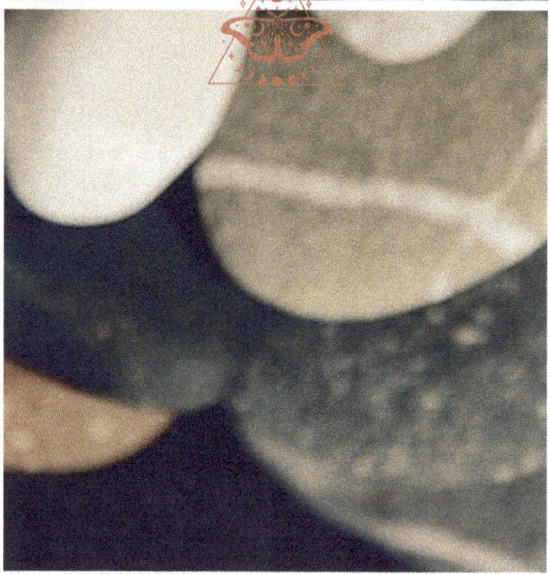

Letting Go of the Pain & Pivoting with Purpose

Loss isn't only felt through the departure of loved ones. Whether parting from a beloved pet, confronting unmet dreams, or saying farewell to a former home, every situation brings unique heartache that we often sweep under the rug. *Have you ever caught yourself minimizing a pain simply because it wasn't about the loss of a person? How did that make you feel?*

Yet, by confronting this pain, we find solace and allow these memories to enrich our grasp of life's profound teachings. *Can you recall when confronting a painful memory brought you unexpected peace or understanding?*

Navigating the intense emotions that follow a significant loss is a challenge. We seek wholesome ways to cope, transcend anguish, and rediscover life's purpose. *What coping strategies have you tried in the past, and which ones felt most genuine to your healing process?*

By immersing ourselves in meditation and mindfulness, we can accept our painful recollections and find healing. This deliberate path calls for dedication, assisting us in reconciling with our losses and seeking avenues for renewed growth. *Do you find solace in stillness and introspection, or does it feel daunting to confront your feelings head-on?*

Moving With, as we let go of what once was and channel our experiences into purpose, we gain clarity. *How has an experience shaped your present purpose or perspective?*

Key Points

- Grief and loss are unique personal experiences that can provoke intense mental, emotional, and physical manifestations.

- Your health, personality, and support can strengthen you to carry your grief and move forward in growth.

- Meditation has always been integral to healing from the trauma of the unexpected loss of a loved one.

- You can come to terms with your loss with time and conscious efforts.

Exercise

Before we start this next exercise together, I want you to be gentle with yourself. Meditation and mindfulness can surface intense memories and emotions, allowing us to work through them and begin our healing journeys. However, if you experience PTSD or painful flashbacks and symptoms, please take a step back, give yourself space, and reach out for help. Our goal is to help you feel safe, mindful, and strong.

You've got this. Follow the prompts below to get started.

01　Find a private, peaceful place to sit comfortably for 10-15 minutes.

02　Get comfortable – you can use pillows, blankets, or other comfort items.

03　Take a deep breath in slowly.

04　Inhale for 5 seconds.

05　Hold for 5 seconds.

06　Exhale for 5 seconds.

07　Repeat five times.

08　Now, shift your breath to your body and mind. Check-in with yourself. It is not good or bad. ––realize how you're feeling from an outside perspective as if you were a loving friend or family member.

09　How is your body feeling? Give it compassion and grace.

 # Exercise

10   How is your mind feeling? Give it empathy and understanding.

11   Now, imagine the loved one you are grieving. Picture the happiest version of their face.

12   If you could say anything to them, think about it or say it aloud. Focus on healing and grace.

13   Now, imagine their response in a loving, kind way. Could you let it be the words you need to hear?

14   Now, let your mind drift into a visualization of a happy memory with them. Allow yourself to experience this memory in your mind entirely.

15   Once ready, shift your focus back to your breath.

16   Take a deep breath in slowly. Inhale for 5 seconds.

17   Hold for 5 seconds.

18   Exhale for 5 seconds.

19   Repeat five times.

20   Slowly open your eyes when ready and reflect on your experiences. Be gentle with yourself for the rest of the day.

The Stages of Grief & The Stages of Grief Alignment

Objective: To understand the five stages of grief, how to heal through your grief using meditation, and move from acceptance to embracing.

The Journey of Grief

Grief. It's such a personal yet almost mysterious word. Even those sitting face-to-face with our grief rarely find the right words to describe it. Experts have whittled it down into a 5-step path to help us better understand this individual yet shared experience:

Five Stages of Grief

Together, we will focus more on the 7 Stages of Grief Alignment. But before we can embrace, we must first understand.

Here's a simple overview of the Five Stages of Grief:

1. Denial: No, this cannot be happening to me.
2. Anger—Why me? Who's blaming? I do not deserve this!
3. Bargaining: Don't do this. Do not, and I will _____!
4. Depression: Life is unfair to me. There is only darkness. I can't handle it anymore.
5. Acceptance: I accept this sudden and unfortunate turn in life. I am at peace with it.

I gently ask you to take a moment and think: Where are you on this journey?

Give yourself grace, as there is no wrong answer now. We can only move *with*, moving forward, pivoting with purpose to embrace the 7 stages of grief alignment.

The Journey of Healing

One of the core elements of healing from trauma is to discover, address, and work through it. Meditation is one of the most potent tools found within us that allows us to confront our grief and move forward with a renewed sense of freedom and love for ourselves and others. Through meditation, you can heal all your wounds and touch on each area of grief, trauma, bullying, and abuse. While it can challenge your mind and heart, meditation trains your awareness. It lets you control your thoughts and eliminate distractions that trigger emotional wandering and habitual negativity.

Whether through breathwork, journaling, or yoga, shifting our awareness to the here and now can allow us to make amends with our past and intentionally pave a healthy future. Reconsidering experiences from this newfound mindset will equip us with clarity to create healthy futures filled with purposeful intent! Take a moment to pause and observe. When you do, there is an opportunity for growth and healing. Accepting your feelings instead of denying them builds strength and courage that can fuel you forward.

Your Next Steps to Acceptance

- Recognize your grief or loss. Consider it from a distance and express empathy to yourself.

- Recognize that you may go through various and unexpected emotional changes.

- Recognize that each person's grief process is unique. There is no 'correct' way to mourn.

- Seek the help and support of others. Seek the advice of a mental health professional if necessary.

- Accept responsibility for your emotional, mental, and physical health.

The Seven Stages
of Grief Alignment

While the Five Stages help us better understand our grief experience, the fifth stage isn't the final. It's the beginning of a new, intentional journey—the journey to embracing The 7 Stages of Grief Alignment saved me. They taught me to embrace, empower, and pivot from pain to purpose.

EXPRESS
Write all your emotions, your heavy feelings, without judgment. Release to find peace.

MEDITATE
Releasing and letting go. Find healing in intention. Open yourself up to the universe and connect your body, mind, and spirit to the healing power of the present moment—heavy feelings without judgment.

BE PRESENT
Stop keeping yourself busy and be still. Breathe in. Breathe out. Carve out moments to release the hustle and allow yourself to *be* in the **POD** - Pause. Observe. Discern.

REJUVENATE
Disconnect to reconnect. Whether going on trips and adventures with friends or reading a book in bed, self-care is sacred. Energize and rejuvenate your soul. Make time for your inner sanctuary. Take control; create moments of peace so you can fully reconnect!

AWAKEN
Practice mindfulness –– observe yourself from a higher, divine perspective. Tune into the PAUSE. Let go of the past and trust in the future. Enjoy the now.

CONNECT
Connect your mind, body, and spirit. Give gratitude, shift to the positive, and meditate on what gives you hope.

EAT HEALTHY
Food is fuel. I'm not saying you should follow a fad diet or restrict yourself. The goal of embracing is to become more in sync with your inner and higher selves. Listen to your body and give it the flavors, nutrients, and energy it needs. You don't have to do it all at once; we're just focused on meditation. Allow yourself to accept and embrace your healing journey, one step at a time.

Key Points

- To heal, you must first acknowledge your feelings. Accept them.

- While the Five Stages help us better understand our grief experience, the fifth stage isn't final. It's the beginning of a new, intentional journey –the journey to embracing.

- There's healing by tuning into your inner world, caring for yourself, and living in the present moment.

 # Exercise

For this chapter's exercise, we will combine the powers of our first two elements of EMBRACE: Express and Meditate. Answer the questions and follow the prompts below. BREATHE, PAUSE in between each moment, and feel all of it.

01 Find a journal and something to write with.

02 Now, permit yourself to express yourself.

03 Tell yourself that there is no judgment here.

04 Now, write all your emotions. Your heavy feelings. Imagine them releasing from your body as you write them down.

05 Be gentle with yourself through this process.

06 Once you've reached the end of your writing flow state, take a step back and breathe.

07 Close your eyes.

08 Breathe in for 5 seconds.

09 Hold for 5 seconds.

10 Breathe out for 5 seconds.

11 Repeat five times, focusing solely on your breath.

Exercise

12 Now, imagine you're observing yourself from outside of your body. Objectively keep the thoughts, emotions, and experiences you wrote.

13 Imagine observing these thoughts as the most loving, understanding person or creature you know. Maybe it's God, a loved one, or even a pet.

14 Imagine yourself as that being; give yourself that grace, nonjudgmental love, support, and embrace you seek.

15 Allow yourself to sit in the warmth and light of this love.

16 Once you're ready, shift your focus back to the present.

17 Breathe in for 5 seconds.

18 Hold for 5 seconds.

19 Breathe out for 5 seconds.

20 When you're ready, open your eyes.

Four Ways to Heal:
Cultivate Positivity, Enrich it, Absorb it, Correlate Positivity & Negativity

Objective: To learn how to use your energy and focus on healing your heart and spirit.

Cultivate Positivity

Our focus shapes our life experiences. By simply spending a moment to discuss the hue of yellow, we can suddenly realize how prevalent this vibrant color is in everyday life —it's not as if more objects have appeared out of thin air; instead, simply by changing how we look at things, new perspectives are a sight to embrace!

Now, this applies to positivity and negativity as well. If you focus on the positive, you'll see more light in your life. If you dwell on the negative, you'll see more shadows.

The journey toward recovery begins with cultivating a positive, uplifting mindset. However, this is far from an effortless endeavor, particularly for those who have suffered multiple traumas or are naturally inclined to look on the darker side of things.

Now is the time to take charge of your mindset by training your brain to appreciate all that's positive in life. Instead of searching far and wide, look closer than you think: it's already within reach! Tap into a feeling full of support and security; this will help bring more joyous experiences to your journey.

Through meditation, we can pause and catch glimpses of the ever-present divine support. Gratitude becomes easier to embody when we give ourselves space for stillness, allowing us to experience all the blessings this world has waiting for us.

Enrich it

It's easy to get bogged down with daily struggles, but what if we took the time to savor and relish our happy moments? Taking a few minutes each day to reflect on these positive memories can help revive your optimism! Try embracing even small, joyful experiences as an opportunity for growth.

Appreciate the beauty that life offers and savor each moment. Let your spirit soar when you receive a compliment, and document special occasions with photographs or memories so they will never be forgotten. Instead of dwelling on difficult times, meditate on your past's positive memories rather than ruminate on the painful ones. How might cherishing the good moments reshape your perspective on the challenges?

Absorb it

Immerse yourself in the bliss of unbridled joy, allowing it to seep into your spirit and touch every aspect of your being. Allow freedom, happiness, and optimism to become a permanent fixture within the depths of your heart—forever positive!

Allow the light of optimism to take away your sorrow and pain; healing heart harmony has brought that low. Embrace the positive facets of life; they'll cast an illuminating glow, fostering internal healing. How might your days change if you consistently nurtured this inner light?

Correlate Positivity & Negativity

Believe that change is calling your name; remove the bad influences from your life to make room for hope. Free yourself from burdens that don't cultivate a space for hope and positivity!

This can mean creating boundaries with people, places, and things that drain you rather than fuel you. Setting clear boundaries with what brings you down can help you release some of the weight of the grief and trauma you carry.

Far from being an avenue for fleeing our trials, meditation can assist us in facing what may feel uncomfortable and unsettling. But rather than simply dwelling on the source of difficulty, it is possible to allow ourselves to accept these awkward elements, eventually realizing that courageous reckoning with such feelings paves a path towards personal growth and healing.

By connecting with your own story, allowing your own experiences, and letting the surrounding beauty fill your soul, you can erase the fearful feelings attached to your painful experience of losing a loved one and cope with that traumatic experience. Give yourself the grace to embrace your hope for yesterday and tomorrow.

Instead of dwelling on less-than-ideal moments, why not focus our attention and energy on positive experiences? Take the time to savor those treasured memories, even if they are tiny sparks of joy. Let's open ourselves up to optimism and enjoy more deeply enriching moments!

Celebrate even the smallest bursts of enthusiasm and build lasting memories for yourself as you go! Instead of dwelling on past hurts, focus your energy on reflecting on fond recollections. Let them bring joy when they come up in thought.

Key Points

- If you focus on the positive, you'll see more light in your life. If you dwell on the negative, you'll see more shadows around you.

- Train your brain to admire the positivity already around you to cultivate positivity. Enrich optimism and deepen your positive experiences–even if they're small.

- Visualize yourself absorbing these moments of light and love.

- Let go of what no longer serves and uplift you to make more room for what does.

Exercise

Moon rituals are ancient practices that allow us to have sacred natural experiences. They inspire healing, intention, and self-love by tuning us into the moon and its many phases. For this chapter's practice, we will perform a moon ritual. The moon's unique phrases remind us that change can be positive and magical.

Releasing and Letting Go:
Forest Bathing

01 Grab a pen and set off on an adventure to find a peaceful spot in nature -- preferably a place with trees, like a forest. Safely go in the evening time so that you can see the moon. Consider inviting a friend or loved one.

02 Find a tree that you feel drawn to and sit beneath it.

03 Write your intentions on the piece of paper. Maybe you intend to cultivate, enrich, and absorb the surrounding light.

04 Now, stand up and look up at the tree. Admire and absorb its beauty. Accept its beauty amidst any of its imperfections.

05 Look up at the moon. Soak in its beauty and let it nourish your acceptance of change, as it, too, goes through many phases.

06 Imagine yourself releasing and letting go of what's weighing on you --your grief, pain, and faulty memories. Imagine them floating to the sky and tucking behind the moon or leaves.

07 Now imagine your intentions glowing within you. Imagine them building and filling your heart and mind, giving you the capacity for positive change and acceptance.

08 When you're ready, take a deep breath.

Creating a Meditation Space for Healing

Objective: To understand the importance of meditating where you feel safe and how to create a meditation space for healing.

Your Environment Affects Your Energy

Even if we aren't aware of it, the people and surroundings around us constantly affect us. Think about how your energy and perception shift in a dark, loud restaurant versus a light, open space outside.

The sounds, sights, and senses attached to our environments stimulate our emotions. This is especially true for empaths, compassionate people, and those who've experienced trauma, grief, and loss.

Notice how your energy shifts in response to different people and places. With increased awareness, you can nurture yourself by surrounding yourself with the things that uplift you!

Meditate Where You Feel Safe & Secure

Meditation is an empowering method to open oneself up and create a safe space to reflect, recover, and build meaningful connections. Before beginning your journey inward, intuitively tune into the environment around you—find a peaceful corner where all your focus can stay on relaxation!

In moments of quiet reflection, we often expose ourselves to the pains and emotions of our past. But meditation is about compassionate acceptance. We are embracing all that has come before without judgment so that it no longer has power over us.

When we create a safe space for this inner work, we can cultivate a more meaningful connection with ourselves through awareness and understanding.

Unplug from the stress of daily life and find your inner peace in a place that lets you EXPRESS, BE PRESENT to appreciate new perspectives, REJUVENATE with some much-needed rest for body and soul, AWAKEN creativity or intuition within yourself through mindful practices, and CONNECT meaningfully to others. Entering this tranquil environment allows one to enjoy an open mindset free from unwanted distractions.

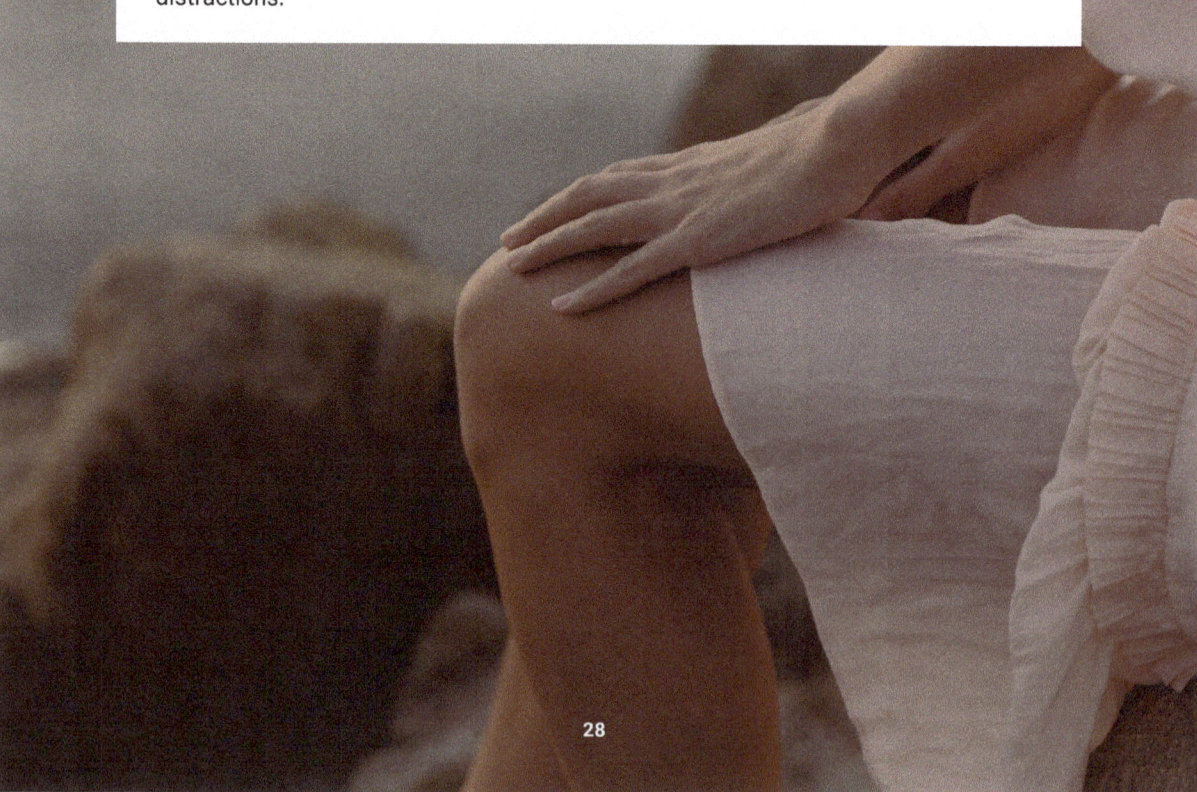

Elements of a Healing Meditation Space

Once you find your space, it's time to make it sacred to you.
Here are some elements of healing environments that might speak to your senses
and make your space one of healing and purpose:

SIGHTS

Enhance your meditation space with candles, tea lights, or salt lamps. Hang paintings, photos, crystals, and other sights that elevate, comfort, and offer you hope if you think it's appropriate for your environment.

SOUNDS

Playing comforting binaural beats creates calm. Solfeggio frequencies are better for relaxing your nerves and settling you into a peaceful slumber. Solfeggio frequencies are nine different frequencies that all have specific health benefits. Become acquainted with frequencies that can promote relaxation, and positivity, and decrease anxiety.

BE PRESENT

Our sense of smell is deeply tied to our emotions. Studies show that our olfactory system has the most robust connection to our memories. Therefore, smelling an old family recipe or walking into your favorite park from childhood can transport you back in time.

Be intentional about the scent of your space with essential oils, candles, or incense.

TOUCH

Placing our hand on our heart while meditating can create a comforting sensation, fostering a deeper connection and cultivating a sense of grounding and presence.

THIS FIRST REQUIRES US TO GET COMFORTABLE.

While meditating, you can lie on a soft cushion or surface. Assemble blankets, pillows, or other comfort items, tuning into your senses for an authentic experience. This is your own personal sanctuary.

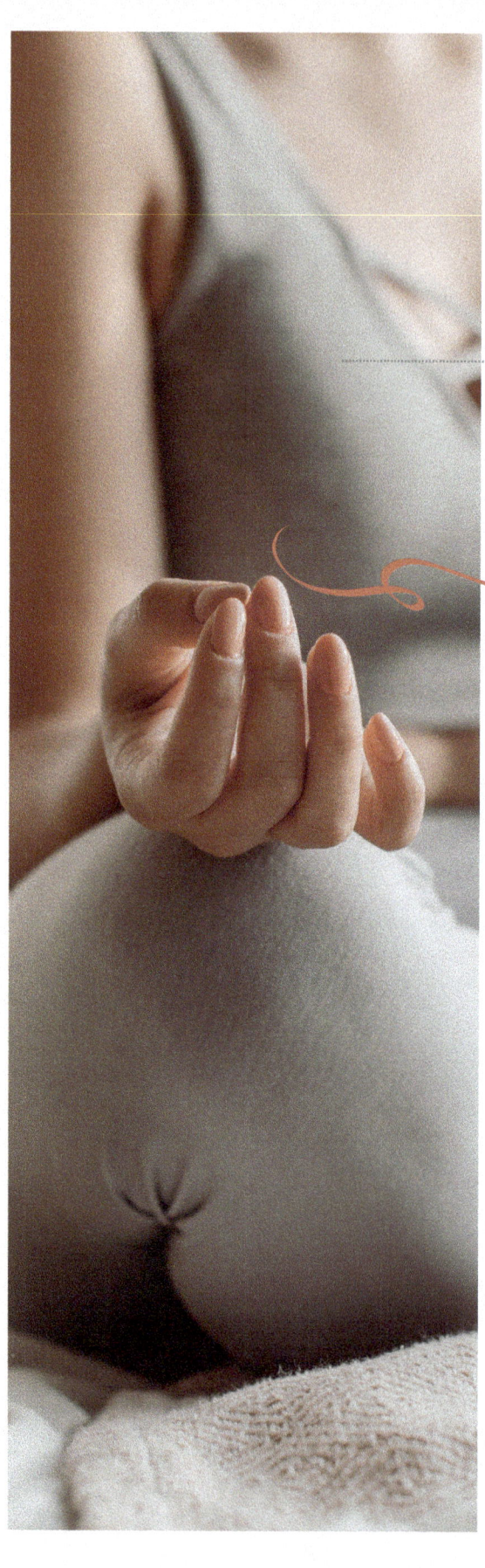

Key Points

- Our emotions are stimulated by the feelings associated with our surroundings. This is especially true for those who've experienced trauma, grief, and loss.

- The best meditation spot is neutral, allowing us to EMBRACE our desire to EXPRESS, BE PRESENT, REJUVENATE, AWARENESS, or CONNECT.

- Create a safe and pleasant environment by purposefully nurturing sights, sounds, fragrances, and touch sensations that feel appropriate for you.

Exercise

Let's set up a safe meditation space unique to YOU. Answer the questions and follow the prompts below to get started.

Grab your pen. We're going to express your feelings for your meditation space.

What sights and visuals uplift you?
Is it the mountains? A picture of loved ones? Lights, crystals, or lamps?

_____

_____

_____

_____

_____

_____

_____

_____

Once you determine those, gather them to form your space.

Now, what sounds uplift you?
Create a meditation playlist of songs or sounds that relax you and bring you comfort.

_____

_____

_____

_____

_____

_____

_____

_____

Next, what scents speak to you?
Whether incense, essential oils, or candles, gather scents that relax and rejuvenate your spirit.

_____

_____

_____

_____

_____

_____

_____

_____

Last, gather comfort items like blankets, pillows, etc., to comfort you by touch.

Once you've created your space, honor it and set it apart
as your sacred meditation space.

a. Get into a comfortable position.

b. Close your eyes. .

c. Take ten deep breaths, in and out.

Healing in Action:
Meditation Exercise for Trauma

Objective: To identify the physical and emotional side effects of carrying unresolved trauma and how meditation can help us work through them

Releasing Unresolved Trauma

Trauma can be an invisible burden, lurking beneath the surface and weighing us down. Unresolved trauma often gets trapped in our bodies—suppressing emotions and resulting in physical symptoms that reflect inner turmoil. Healing from this suffering requires understanding how it lingers within us so that we may regain control over ourselves.

Although we often prioritize physical healing, the truth is that emotional wounds can be equally impactful on our overall health and happiness. Caring for our mental well-being should never take a back seat when cultivating inner peace.

To achieve true healing, we must first open ourselves up to awareness - taking the time to acknowledge our physical, mental, and emotional states. This enlightened voyage of self-discovery is required for everyone to undergo a healing metamorphosis.

Physical Wounds of Unresolved Trauma	Emotional Wounds of Unresolved Trauma
• Physical stiffness and rigidity • Poor digestion • Insomnia • Restlessness	• Poor emotional health • Slow responses • High sensitivity • Hyperarousal • Imbalance in attitude and behavior toward everything • Lack of concentration • Low self-esteem Disassociation

Meditation to Move with the Trauma of Losing Your Love One

Unresolved trauma can become an invisible sickness, damaging our mental and physical health until we feel completely immobilized. But there is still hope. Rather than pretending it never happened or burying it, working through the pain will result in profound healing.

We can reprogram our minds through contemplative practice to manifest contentment and joy. Meditation provides a powerful toolkit for facing life's challenges with resilient positivity rather than remaining restricted by past traumas or negativity. It allows us to confront difficult experiences openly yet compassionately—equipping us with the resources to survive and thrive!

Meditation can provide a pathway to healing from trauma, but the journey has challenges. Along with moments of connection and inner peace come vulnerability, discomfort, and sometimes painful memories that must be faced head-on before actual progress can be made.

Healing trauma can intimidate, but don't let it scare you away --we're here to heal. So take a deep breath and have faith in yourself as you rediscover experiences that may have been forgotten or buried deep inside you. Let's journey to restore balance and find peace within ourselves.

Extend yourself the grace you so willingly give others.

Key Points

- Unresolved trauma gets stuck into your physical body, restricting and blocking your emotions.

- We profoundly affect our mental peace and physical well-being by tending to our emotional wounds.

- Meditation helps you rewire your brain for joy and happiness and endure traumatic experiences.

- It's not painless −−but there's no need to be scared. It's all about grace, healing, and self-love.

Exercise

For this chapter's exercise, we're going to practice mindfulness. Mindfulness is a gentle, accessible way to gain the benefits of meditation, especially for those of us carrying unresolved trauma. Together, follow the prompts below:

01

Get into your safe meditation space and make yourself comfortable.

02

Once you're ready, close your eyes and draw attention to your breath.

03

Notice the natural flow of your regular breath. Notice the breath flow into your nose, fill your lungs, and rush back out. Extend thanks to your body for how naturally and effortlessly it does this for you.

04

After a few natural breaths, take one deep breath through your nose, counting from 1, 2, 3, 4, and 5.

05

Once you've fully inhaled, hold your breath for 1, 2, 3, 4, and 5. Notice how your lungs feel fully expanded.

06

Now exhale through your nose, 1, 2, 3, 4, 5.

07

Repeat this process 5-10 more times, paying attention to the sensations in your body. Pay attention to the movement and expansion of your lungs. Notice the cool air traveling down your throat on the inhale and the warm hair leaving your body on the exhale.

08

If you get distracted, don't worry. Gently shift your focus back to your bodily sensations. Get in tune with how you're feeling at this very moment.

09

After 5-10 deep breaths, practice this 5-10 more times, but this time, I want you to...

a.Imagine your body filling with light and healing on every inhale.

b.And on every hold, I want you to imagine the oxygen traveling through your veins, drawing out all the tension, resistance, and pain you've held onto.

c.On the exhale, I want you to imagine this tension and pain traveling up and leaving your body, disappearing as soon as it releases.

d.As you continue inhaling and exhaling, more and more light replaces this pain, and soon enough, your body and mind are glowing with light.

10

Once you've finished your practice, allow yourself to shift back to your natural breath and breathe in and out five times. When you're ready, open your eyes.

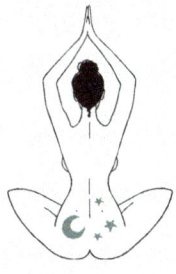

Meditation Techniques to Transition Purposefully Using the Body Scan Method

Objective: To understand the power of connecting with your body and honoring your needs of body scanning.

Checking in with YOU

Life is busy! And if you're a Heyoka Empath like me, you might take on others' emotions and needs as you move about your day. While caring for others is a beautiful, transformative gift, we must not forget to care for ourselves.

Self-care isn't selfish. Remember: You can't pour from an empty cup. It's time to fill it together (and even let it overflow!).

Checking in with yourself can be as simple as asking how you're doing daily. It can enlighten you with the ability to tune into and connect your body, mind, and spirit. As we go through the busyness of our days, it's almost easy to feel separated from our bodies, running on autopilot and going through the motions. This is incredibly tempting for those with heavy grief and loss.

Many trauma survivors feel alienated and dissociated from their bodies as if they observe and watch their life happen to them.

However, checking in with ourselves, connecting with our bodies, and expressing our feelings allows us to move through them. It fortifies us to build a lovely garden with our grieving tears and thrives our purpose out of agony. Meditation is all about becoming comfortable with the uncomfortable to EMBRACE and EMPOWER ourselves.

Check-in with you. Please be aware of your needs and honor them.

You are always deserving of this necessary yet transformational act of self-love.

The Body Scan Method

Body scanning is a mindfulness meditation practice focusing awareness on various body areas systematically and nonjudgmentally. Body scanning is intended to promote a deep sense of bodily awareness, which can aid in the release of tension and stress, increase relaxation, and develop a stronger connection with the present moment. Typically, a body scan begins with the feet and progresses gently through the legs, chest, arms, and head, paying attention to each body region.

As we bring attention to each area, one may notice sensations such as warmth, tingling, or tightness, and the goal is to observe these sensations without trying to change them. Body scanning can be useful for reducing anxiety, improving sleep, and boosting general well-being with frequent practice.

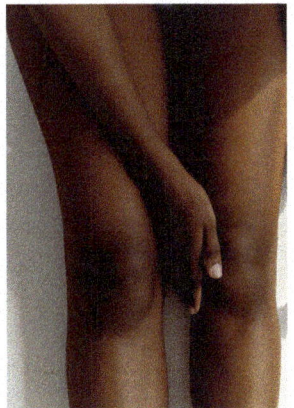  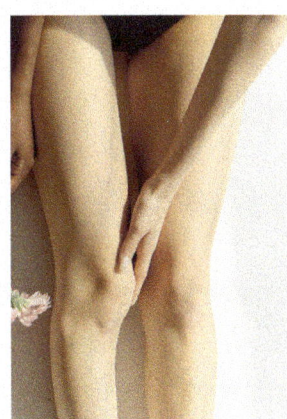

Body scanning seeks to reconnect and harmonize the mind and body. To speak with and be empowered by our bodies. Body scanning can bring you into the present moment. It might disclose what you require and how you should care for yourself now. It enables us to transition from autopilot to waking up to the beauty of the present moment.

Ultimately, the choice between body scanning and other types of meditation depends on preference and individual needs. Both methods can effectively promote mindfulness and enhance overall well-being, and individuals may benefit from incorporating both practices into their self-care routine.

All you need is 5 minutes each day. Let go of the chains of the past and future, let go of your to-do list, and let go of your need to make sure everyone else's cup is full for just a moment and take care of yourself—Check in with yourself.

Key Points

- Self-care isn't selfish.

- It's easy to feel separated from our bodies, running on autopilot and going through the motions.

- Checking in with ourselves, connecting with our bodies, and expressing these emotions empower us to move through them.

- Body scanning is mindfulness meditation that brings awareness to each body part.

- Bring your awareness to the here and now and shift your focus to what you need and how you can care for yourself today.

 **Exercise**

QUIZ

What does self-care mean to you?

_____
_____
_____
_____

How can body scanning help us take care of ourselves through our grief?

_____
_____
_____
_____

JOURNAL PROMPTS

How is your body feeling today?

_____
_____
_____
_____
_____
_____
_____

What might that tension be from, physically?

_____

_____

_____

_____

What might that tension be from, emotionally?

_____

_____

_____

_____

What part(s) of your body feel strong, relaxed, or powerful?

_____

_____

_____

_____

What might you be doing to help them feel that way?

_____

_____

_____

_____

Action Prompt

We're going to practice body scanning together. Find your safe meditation space, get comfortable, lie or sit down, and follow the prompts below.

01 Find a comfortable and quiet place to lie down on your back with your arms at your sides and your legs slightly apart. You can also sit in a chair if lying down is uncomfortable.

02 Close your eyes and take a few deep breaths, allowing your body to relax and your mind to become more focused.

03 Bring attention to your feet, noticing warmth, tingling, or tension. Spend a few moments focusing on your feet before moving to the next part of your body.

04 Slowly move your attention up through your legs, paying attention to any sensations in your calves, knees, thighs, and hips.

05 Continue to move your attention up through your torso, paying attention to your lower back, abdomen, chest, and upper back.

06 Move your attention to your arms, starting with your hands and moving up through your forearms, upper arms, and shoulders.

07 Finally, bring your attention to your head and neck, noticing any sensations in your face, jaw, neck, and scalp.

08 As you move through each part of your body, try to observe any sensations without judgment or analysis. Notice them and let them be.

09 Once you have completed the body scan, take a few moments to rest and be with any sensations that arise in your body.

10 When you're ready, slowly open your eyes and bring your attention back to the present moment.

You can practice this exercise for as long as you like, starting with a few minutes and gradually increasing the time as you become more comfortable with the practice.

Rituals for Remembrance:
Rite of Passage Moon Meditation

Objective: To explore the meaning of rituals and how you can create meditative rituals to remember, honor, and connect with your loved ones.

The Power of Rituals

Our journey has been filled with knowledge and inspiration, so let's take it further. Hold my hand as we harness your newfound wisdom to heal, strengthen relationships, and set daily goals through transformative rituals. Let's ignite your path to growth and fulfillment.

Repetition is powerful. Routine has the power to transform. When we cultivate attentive habits and uphold our healing rituals, we demonstrate to ourselves and the Universe that we are open to receiving—that we are willing to do whatever it takes to give our pain a purpose and tend to our gardens of grief.

Through rituals, we can remember and honor those who have passed away while also planting a loving seed of recollection in our souls. Incorporating these techniques into our daily lives fosters compassion in ourselves, allowing us to better recall and heal from loss.

It's all about intention with EMBRACE. It's about claiming the life we know we deserve—the life we know we're capable of—right now.

To help you create rituals of celebration and remembrance, I will energetically guide you so that you can connect with your loved ones, your past selves, and your energetic, endless future.

Moon Rituals

Like the moon, we go through phases and times of brightness and darkness in our lives. The beauty is that no matter what misfortune comes our way or how difficult things appear, something will always stand firm, as the stable moon does throughout its cycles, never changing.

This balance of constancy and change can ground us in our journeys through the next chapters of our life without the actual presence of our loved ones. While our pain and grief may ebb and flow, the constancy of hope for healing and the spiritual presence of our loved ones never change.

Moon rituals—meditations that tap into our mysterious celestial sanctuary's different phases and energies—can help you harness the power of lunar energy. Step away from your everyday routine and join Mother Moon on an exhilarating meditation adventure!

- When the moon waxes, you can create your ritual based on its manifestation and expansive energy. Manifest your future by journaling, meditating, and acting in abundance.

- When the moon wanes, you can honor your ritual and intention based on releasing, boundaries, and letting go. Could you let go of what no longer serves you? Write these words down, throw them away, take a warm bath, or even dance away the negative energy!

- When the moon is full, its energy is high, and you can find peace as you exhale and feel whole. Practice self-care and declutter your life of what might hold you back. You can even use the healing powers of rainwater to cleanse your energy.

Key Points

- When we create mindful habits and honor our healing routines, we show ourselves and the Universe that we're open to receiving.

- The moon is symbolic of our journey here on Earth. We go through phases, seasons, and moments of lightness, darkness, of feeling whole or incomplete.

- This balance of constancy and change can ground us in our journeys. While our pain and grief may ebb and flow, the endurance of hope for healing and the spiritual presence of our loved ones never changes.

- Waxing Moon Energy = Manifestation and abundance. Waning Moon Energy = Releasing.

- Full Moon = Cleansing and letting go.

Exercise

Why are rituals so powerful?

_____
_____
_____
_____

Why is the moon symbolic of our life journeys?

_____
_____
_____
_____

JOURNAL PROMPTS

How can you make meditation a ritual of remembrance and celebration of your loved one's life?

_____
_____
_____
_____
_____
_____
_____
_____

What would you like to manifest and invite into your life during the Waxing Moon Energy?

_____
_____
_____
_____

What would you like to release and let go of in your life during the Waning Moon Energy?

_____
_____
_____
_____

What would you like to cleanse and care for in your life during the Full Moon?

_____
_____
_____
_____

Action Prompt

Thank You for Choosing You.

You take a powerful step toward self-discovery by starting your recovery and creating your own self-modalities during prayer or meditation.

May the force of optimism guide you, may a purpose that both enlightens and inspires fuel your days and may you experience unparalleled growth on this path that was never our choosing.

You are, without a doubt, deserving of all life has to offer.

The Grief Warrior

What does the word EMBRACE mean to you?

To me, embracing empowers.

Embracing is a step beyond acceptance.
We must first accept our grief to healing and embrace it.
Our grief is where authentic alignment happens.

It's where we find the purpose for our pain, growth in our grief, and life after loss.

It's where everything clicks, and it all makes sense.

That's what The 7 Stages of Grief is all about EMBRACE.
I can't wait for you to experience 'BE PRESENT in our next stage' and embrace the transformative 'Pivot with PAUSE' modality!

Make that leap of faith.

You Got This!

Michele C. Bell's narrative is a profound testament to resilience, the transformative power of embracing life's most profound challenges, and the depth of human compassion. Her journey, which began with the deeply personal and original work "*A Journey of Unconditional Love*," evolved into the 22-time award-winning story, "*A Son's Gift*," marking the inception of her distinguished career as an empathetic voice within the realm of grief literature.

With a Ph.D. in Philosophy and Metaphysics, Michele brings a unique blend of intuitive insight and scholarly depth to "*The 7 Stages of Grief* - **EMBRACE**." This work, unlike traditional grief literature, opens a space where healing is interwoven with personal growth and transformation, guided by Michele's own experiences, her profound journey through PTSD, and her scholarly insights. This journey has not only deepened her understanding of grief and resilience but also infused her writing with authenticity and compassion, offering solace and a transformative roadmap to those navigating the intricacies of loss.

Her innovative approach, blending the profound depths of intuitive philosophy with avant-garde grief counseling modalities, pioneers a novel paradigm in grief literature. Michele's work, transcending meticulous writing and exploration, charts a path towards transformative healing. Each stage, encapsulated within the evocative acronym **EMBRACE**, is meticulously crafted to guide the bereaved with dignity, offering nuanced understanding through the labyrinth of loss.

Beyond her literary contributions, Michele's life story—marked by resilience amidst adversity—enriches her professional narrative. From facing challenges such as bullying and domestic abuse to navigating the complexities of being a holistic real estate broker, Michele's experiences underscore her innate desire to support individuals through significant life transitions. The profound loss of her son to Ewings Sarcoma tested her resolve, catalyzing a shift towards mental health advocacy and the development of groundbreaking methodologies like the Soul Design technique and the *7 Stages of Grief* workbooks.

Michele's contributions extend to her active involvement in suicide prevention and domestic abuse programs, where her voice has become a force for change. Her purpose, whether as a holistic real estate broker, end-of-life expert, or mental health advocate, remains consistent—to support, guide, and uplift. As a member and keynote speaker for the **Daughters of Penelope**, Michele shares inspiring messages of healing, humor, and love, emphasizing the necessity of such virtues in today's world.

At 58, Michele C. Bell, The Grief Warrior®, stands as a testament to the enduring power of the human spirit, commanding respect and fostering deep, authentic connections. Her life experiences, granting her the invaluable CAT credentials of **Compassion, Authenticity, and Trust**, continue to inspire those fortunate enough to encounter her legacy..

Testimonial

In the wake of losing my niece, who was both an integral part of our family business and my daily life, I was engulfed by survivor's guilt and a maelstrom of emotions. At 74, having built a successful business career, I was unprepared for the profound impact this tragedy would have. The accident that took her life left me alone with my grief and a host of unresolved feelings, including an intense rage and sadness.

Then, I encountered Michele. She introduced me to a world of grace and dignity I hadn't known was possible. She guided me through techniques to stay ahead of depression, reduce stress, and embrace the present—prayer, meditation, and deep, conscious breathing became part of my routine. Her 30-day challenges and the comprehensive support she provided, spanning personal loss to business strategies, were transformative.

But Michele's impact didn't stop there. She introduced me to her eating healthy modality—incorporating balanced diets, regular exercise, and supplements into my daily regimen. These changes, under her guidance, not only improved my mental clarity but also led to significant weight loss and helped me stop drinking. Michele's approach broke me down and rebuilt me, a process my family witnessed as I underwent these massive shifts.

This woman has led me to a profound state of gratitude. Through her encouragement to write letters and share my deepest thoughts in a safe and authentic space, I found a unique kind of healing. Michele has restored joy to my life, demonstrating that even at this age, profound transformation is possible. Her expertise and genuine presence have given me back to myself, and family healthier and more vibrant. I stand in humble acknowledgment of the incredible journey she has guided me through.

Mike

DISCLAIMER

All content within the 7 Stages of Grief Alignment Workbook is original and intended solely to promote mind, body, and spirit well-being. This material does not replace the expertise or advice of a licensed mental health professional. Grief experiences are unique to each individual, and while the workbook provides supportive tools and perspectives, it does not guarantee specific outcomes. If you are experiencing intense or extreme distress, please consult a professional.

By using this course, you acknowledge and accept these terms and conditions. The 7 Stages of Grief certification program, conceived and developed by Dr. Michele Bell, offers an innovative, holistic, and empathy-driven approach to understanding and navigating grief. It is rooted in comprehensive research and deep insight into the human experience of loss and recovery.

Program Overview:
- Embracing Growth in Grief: Recognize the transformative potential within grief.
- The 7 Stages of Grief: Explore the intricate emotional journey of grief, encompassing its multifaceted seven stages.
- Pivoting with Purpose: Equip yourself with practical tools to channel grief's raw energy into purposeful action.
- Understanding the Power of Resistance: Gain insights into the obstacles resistance can pose on the healing journey and learn strategies to address and overcome it.
- Coping Modalities: Discover and apply various coping methods tailored to individual grief journeys or to assist others on this path.
- Certification: As a culmination, the program offers a certification examination to ensure a comprehensive understanding of the 7 Stages of Grief methodology.

Engage with the 7 Stages of Grief, All-In-One Master Compilation program to acquire a compassionate and informed approach to navigating the intricate labyrinth of grief, whether for personal growth or as a professional commitment.

Remember, every voice matters in bringing light to the shadows of grief. By uniting, we can raise awareness and create a world where everyone feels understood and supported during their moments of profound loss. I deeply appreciate your commitment to this cause. Please take a moment to sign the **Loss Awareness Day** petition on **Change.org**, inspired by the heartfelt endeavors of Lisa Marie Presley. Together, we can make a difference.
With heartfelt gratitude and hope,
MiMi + The Grief Warrior ®